My Leather Life

Early Years

Peter S. Fiske

Narrated by Thomas V. Peterson

My Leather Life

Early Years

by Peter S. Fiske

narrated by Thomas V. Peterson

Fair Page Media LLC
Springfield, PA

ISBN: 978-0-9989098-4-4

Copyright © 2019 Peter S. Fiske and Thomas V. Peterson

All rights reserved.

Front Cover Photo: Koalas MC Group Photo taken at a club run in the Santa Cruz Mountains, October 1967, *the Henri Leleu Collection, Courtesy of Gay, Lesbian, Bisexual, Transgender Historical Society.* Peter Fiske is in the front row, far right.

to Nomad and Jimmy

to Don and Coulter

to our Brothers in The 15 Association and Delta

to all our Leather Brothers,

Past, Present and Future

Table of Contents

Preface 1

Chapter 1: Youth 5

Chapter 2: Military 17

Chapter 3: Young Leatherman In New York 25

Chapter 4: Young Leatherman In San Francisco 35

Chapter 5: Motorcycle Clubs and Runs 49

Chapter 6: Drag Queens, Hippies, And Drugs 59

Photographs 73

Chapter 7: Stonewall And Spiritual Growth 81

Chapter 8: Maturing As A Leatherman 93

Chapter 9: Whips, Whipping,

       and the Power Exchange 107

Chapter 10: A Leather Brotherhood 121

Epilogue 139

PREFACE

by Thomas V. Peterson

Although I had met Peter Fiske at earlier gatherings of leathermen, I got to know him well at Bootcamp in June 2010. Boy Kevin had agreed to serve me as my "boy" during this four-day leather encampment. We had a play scene that ended with my inserting an ass-hook held in place with a metal cock ring. I told him that only a Fraternal member of The 15 Association could remove it. Then I left camp to get some needed supplies in Ukiah.

Peter Fiske approached me when I returned to camp. "Your boy Kevin enjoys being the center of attention. Your order that he find a Fraternal was a great choice, and it got him to know us better, too."

"Yes," I laughed, "I'm sure he milked the situation for all it was worth."

"I took care of him. Of course, I told him that he owed me some service. With your permission I'll collect by having Kevin serve me for a couple of hours."

That was the start of a deep friendship between Peter and me. We enjoyed BDSM* in a playful, yet intense way. Surprises were part of the fun. As we talked I discovered other similarities. We both believed that gay men should explore their dreams and fantasies, especially to break through

---

*BDSM is an acronym for bondage/discipline, dominance/submission, sadism/masochism.

artificial social boundaries. In the course of our conversations, I told him that I had published an ethnographic essay on gay men's spiritual experiences in the leather community and was writing a historical essay on how spirituality became associated with BDSM for some leathermen. Peter was interested and encouraged me to keep writing. Over time he shared some of his own spiritual experiences as both Top and bottom.

I listened to Peter's stories about the leather world of San Francisco in the 1960s. His memories were priceless and needed to be recorded and preserved. I eventually asked him whether he would become a resource for an essay on the early leather community. My conversations with Peter, Thom Magister, Len Griffith, and others who were leathermen in the 1950s and 1960s had led me to believe that the beginnings of the leather community were more diverse and complex than the myths of the "Old Guard" made it seem. Peter said he would be happy to cooperate. So at the Delta Run on September 5, 2016, I began recording Peter's early experiences among leathermen. He wanted me to have a context for his decision to go to San Francisco in 1968, so he began talking about his youth, military service, and sexual experiences in the Empire Theatre in New York.

I had begun recording Peter's memories, but I wasn't sure how I would use them. Was this to become an essay on the "Old Guard" in San Francisco? How would I limit the project? At the very least, I could transcribe the tapes and give them to the Leather Museum and Archives. I would call Peter from time to time to get more details. For example, he had initially only told me that when he was fourteen years old, he and his friend Barry would tie each other up, beat each other with belts, and occasionally suck each other's dicks. So I prodded. "Where did you play?" I then learned about the little secluded alley where they played outside. "What led you to do this?" He then told me about going to movies and seeing Alan Ladd tied up in the movie *Botany Bay*. He mentioned that he and Barry would see cliffhangers before the main feature, where heroes were tied up and left to die in some burning building. I kept digging. Searching the Internet I found a 1950s serial entitled *Man with a Steel Whip*. It would be too good to be true if Peter actually saw that one! When I asked, he said he definitely remembered seeing it. Soon the episode of Peter and Barry tying each other up became a rather racy and detailed story.

I approached the project as an artist. I wanted to get as close to the factual truth as possible, but I also wanted a textured story that was interesting to read and explored deeper aspects of life. That meant prodding Peter's memories. My own knowledge of the leather world supplemented some of the background, and my memories usually dovetailed with Peter's. Once, after reading part of the manuscript to him, he said, "I can't believe you're so much in my head." Occasionally, of course, I had to re-write an episode so it conformed more accurately to Peter's memories.

At some point we realized that together we were organizing the facts of Peter's life into narrated stories. By scripting his stories, we were not only recording them but also creating memories from the historical facts of his life. Peter suggested we acknowledge this by making him the author and me the narrator.

Peter's extraordinary life and remarkable character kept me interested in writing these memoirs. His gay leather life merged with many other historical movements: civil rights, hippies, counter-culture spirituality, and AIDS activism. Of course, he was a central actor in fashioning a gay leather world of BDSM and brotherhood.

As I wrote Peter's memoirs, I found stories that exemplified his character: Peter as risk taker, as fighter for people's rights, as caretaker, as explorer, and more. He insisted that the memoirs be an honest reflection of his life. He wanted me to write about his flaws: "warts" as he calls them. These memoirs are not the tales of a saint, but of an unconventional man who lived life to the fullest and helped create the world of leather that we know today.

Both Peter and I want to thank two men who have been extraordinarily supportive and helpful. My slave Jimmy has helped me edit the text to get rid of superfluous words, paragraphs, and sections. When I got stuck and couldn't make something work, he honestly told me what was wrong and how I could make improvements. Our editor, Joel Manon, has encouraged us every step of the way. He helped us choose photographs, create a cover design, and put the manuscript on a fast track for publishing.

Chapter 1: YOUTH

When I was thirteen years old, I remember hiding and watching my brother and his friend Jimmy having jerk-off sessions. They would go to my brother's room, and as they played with themselves, they talked about messing around with girls. I wasn't at all interested in girls, but Jimmy was very handsome and I thought about how much fun it would be to mess around with him. One day they saw me hiding, and my brother said, "Come on in if you want to and play with your own dick." So I joined them, and that was my first orgasm.

About that same time, April 1958, I met Barry, who became my best childhood friend. Barry and I were always together and went to each other's houses or were off exploring together. We were thirteen years old and had lots of exciting adventures together in New York City. Only a couple of months after we met, in the early summer, Barry and I sneaked off to Manhattan together without asking permission from our parents. A Japanese tourist took our picture, then asked for my address, and later sent the picture to me. I still have a photo of the two of us together on the 86th floor of the Empire State Building. We didn't get home until after eight o'clock that night, and our parents were very angry. Barry was grounded for a couple of weeks, while my father gave me a good thrashing.

Barry and I often went to movies together. Both of us were fascinated with scenes of bondage and whipping. When we watched these scenes, I got sexually excited and I'm sure Barry did too. Our neighborhood theatre had an inexpensive Saturday matinee, and at the beginning of each main feature there were short newsreels and a serial cliffhanger. That was designed to get the kids to come to the movie theatre every weekend. Each episode would end with the hero in some predicament where escape seemed impossible. I remember one segment that ended with the hero bound and gagged in a burning building with no apparent way to avoid death. All week long we talked about how he would escape. We would discuss how well he was bound, and that eventually led to our own experimentation with bondage. Some of the action serials took place in a jungle, others on the high seas with pirates and buccaneers. Many were Western serials, and I remember one in particular, *Man with a Steel Whip*, that began my fascination with whips and whipping.

My first memory of going to a movie was in 1953, when I was eight years old. It was *Botany Bay* starring Alan Ladd. My body thrilled with excitement when Ladd was roped to the mast and whipped. Not only was I strongly attracted to handsome men like Alan Ladd, but I also remember shivering when he was given fifty lashes. I imagined myself tied to the mast, whipped, and tortured by sweaty, muscular men. Fear mingled with desire as I imaginatively felt the cat-o'-nine-tails biting into my skin. In retrospect, I'm sure that I felt some kind of prepubescent sexual excitement. Bondage, whipping, and torture were frequent themes in lots of other movies at that time. Villains tied up and tortured heroes in popular Western movies and television shows.

I also remember my parents taking my brother and me to a restaurant called Bronco Charlie's. I don't remember what we ate, but I certainly remember Bronco Charlie (Charlie Miller, 1850-1955). I was 9 and he was 104 years old, a lean, wiry man who was still performing. It is difficult to separate the historical facts of his life from the mythology he created around it. The most certain historical fact is that he was in the Buffalo Bill *Wild West Show* that performed around the nation and at Queen Victoria's Golden Jubilee in 1887 at Windsor Castle in England. A more disputed autobiographical claim is that he was the youngest rider for the Pony Express at eleven years of age. Though his age would have disqualified him, he could have pretended to be older and actually have been one of the riders as he claimed. Almost all the riders were teenagers.

I saw his show at least a half dozen times. He would crack his bullwhip at a girl who had a cigarette in her mouth and put the fire out with the tip of his whip. He would throw twelve knives at another girl and outline her body. In a historical allusion to William Tell, he used a gun to shoot an apple off a girl's head, and like Annie Oakley used a mirror to shoot behind him at a target, always hitting the bull's eye. After the show he would allow me to hold his bullwhip and touch his knives. He even took me on his lap and told me stories about hunting buffalo, described his interactions with Indians, and reminisced about his days in the *Wild West Show*. I loved that old man and have never forgotten his stories — or his bullwhip.

One summer day when we were thirteen, Barry came over to my house. We were alone for the whole afternoon, and I suggested that we tie each other up to see whether or not we could escape. He immediately agreed. After he tied me up, I strained against the ropes trying to escape and got instantly aroused. The more I struggled, the harder my dick got. Since we hadn't really learned any rope-tying techniques yet, I was able to slip out of Barry's first attempt at binding me, though I remained more sexually excited than in any of the jerk-off sessions with my brother and Jimmy.

Then it was my turn to tie him up. I bound his hands behind his back so he couldn't get out — or maybe he didn't try very hard. I decided to scare him a little and took off his belt, doubled it, and threatened to spank his butt. He dared me to do it. So I pulled his bound hands up behind his back until he had to kneel on the floor with his head down and his butt up. With the other hand I swung the belt and landed a few hard blows. I thought of the beatings I had gotten from my father.

In those days most parents spanked their kids to make them behave. My dad disciplined us with his belt until I was nearly fifteen. The last time he whipped me, our friend Jimmy, my brother, and I had chased each other around the house, shooting whipped cream out of cans and making a huge mess. My dad was very angry when he got home. He immediately sent Jimmy home, took off his belt, grabbed me, and started swinging. That time I think my father noticed that the whipping was arousing me, because he stopped before it had gone on very long and said that we were old enough to clean up the mess and that we'd better get at it. The house had better be clean, he threatened, or he would teach both of us a lesson that we wouldn't forget. Jimmy was banned from our house for two or three weeks. That was the last whipping I got from my father.

When my father whipped me, he never bound me nor pulled down my pants, but after hitting Barry a few times on his jeans, I was very sexually excited and without much thought, I quickly pulled him to a standing position, stripped off his pants and underwear, and gave him a few good licks with the belt. He squirmed, yelped, and twisted away, but his dick was hard. I grabbed it and he exploded. Then I pulled down my pants, played with my dick, and quickly shot my load. That was the first jerk-off session I had with Barry.

The next time we played he tied me up, stripped me, and beat my ass with my belt. I found it as exciting to be tied up, whipped, and played with as I did when I tied him up and beat him. Every stroke of the belt would send waves of excitement and energy through me. He laughed as he stroked me and easily made me cum. Very early in my life sexual arousal was linked to whipping and bondage.

Barry and I continued to play, binding each other with ropes, and whipping each other with belts. Our play got more intricate. We found a book in the library on tying knots, and through experimentation became quite good at tying each other's hands, and sometimes feet, together — fairly simple rope bondage, but tight enough so we couldn't escape. Occasionally, we'd also wrap rope around our arms and chests.

Whenever we were sure that we would be alone, we would go to each other's houses to play. But we usually couldn't count on being alone, so that limited our play periods. Eventually we found an abandoned weedy place between two buildings a couple of blocks away that had only one entrance and was quite secluded. It was against a schoolyard fence, and it became our hideout. We were pretty sure that we were safe, because it was off the beaten path and no one could easily see us there. Playing outside added excitement, because there was always the possibility of discovery.

We played these games of bondage, whipping, and sex for well over a year. We invented the scenarios, often inspired by scenes we'd seen on television or in the movies. Our play always involved Dominance and forced submission. It was both forbidden and hot. We would often try to terrorize each other during these scenes, but we always knew we were just playing. Although the scenes involved beatings, we somehow knew each other's limits, and while we pushed those limits, we never really exceeded them. At some point we went beyond just stroking each other's dicks. I don't remember which of us initiated cock sucking, but I think it happened when one of us had the other tied up and forced him to suck dick. Sometimes the boy in charge would frustrate the one tied up by taking him almost to climax, but then not letting him cum — what is now called "edging" in the BDSM community.

On one occasion when we were almost fifteen years old, we explored a place called Uncle Sam's Umbrella Shop. They did sell umbrellas, but the store's main items were riding crops, whips, and canes. When we first visited the shop, the owner wouldn't sell us any of these items. He may have feared that it was some kind of a police set-up. When we went back a second time, he relented and sold us what we wanted. He probably just wanted to get rid of us. That's how we acquired a small stash of whipping implements, which we hid near one of the buildings.

Clearly, my sexual feelings were connected to bondage and whipping that took place within a relationship of Dominance and submission. Barry and I had shared such intimate and exciting moments that it seemed we would be friends forever. We hadn't played with these items more than a few times, however, before we were discovered. We thought our hideout was our exclusive spot, safe from outsiders; we had safely played there for at least a year and a half. But one day, when I had just turned fifteen years old, we were discovered. I don't know for sure who saw us playing in our hiding place and told on us. But that evening our parents confronted us. They not only knew that we were binding and whipping each other, but also that our play involved sex.

Everything happened so fast that it has become a blur in my mind. You can imagine Barry's and my terror at being discovered. Barry's parents came over to our house and both sets of parents confronted us, making us feel that we had done the most horrendous thing possible. Unlike my parents' usual way of physically disciplining me, this time they used shaming. Although my memory is quite fuzzy about details, I still remember the terror of that moment when my father confronted me. I trembled, feeling faint. My mind became a fog, so that I didn't even hear all the words that my parents said. Both families made it clear that Barry and I were not to see each other or even talk to one another again. We passed each other a few times on the street, but never acknowledged each other's presence. Very soon Barry and his parents moved away to another town.

I'm pretty sure my father and mother knew at that time that I was gay — though there was no such positive word then for being homosexual. I am very lucky that they always loved and supported me, though I'm sure they hoped that some day I would straighten out. They probably hoped that if they could keep Barry and me totally separated, then we'd both somehow change as we grew older. I don't know whether Barry had positive support from his family, but I eventually did from mine. I wish that I knew what happened to Barry, but I have lost total contact with him. We had had very positive and wonderful times together despite the traumatic ending.

My family was Catholic, which added a religious element to their discovery and condemnation of my play with Barry. I had gone to St. Aloysius Catholic grade school and was just starting my freshman year at St. Agnes High School when my parents confronted Barry and me. Despite the church's teaching, I hadn't really thought about the jerk-off sessions as serious sins. Of course, there was a forbidden quality about them, but that created more excitement than guilt. My brother never seemed to have any guilt about his jerk-off sessions with Jimmy, and he was my role model. He and Jimmy used the sessions to fantasize about girls, and maybe that made it all right for them. Though I wasn't attracted to girls, I didn't really see any difference in my sexual play with Barry.

When my parents discovered what we were doing, their shock and disapproval finally forced me to face how others viewed sexual acts between boys. For the first time, I was emotionally confronted with the fact that others felt this was a grievous matter. My parents assumed that I would go to confession, and I did. That was the first and only time that I confessed playing sexually with anyone. The Irish priest lectured me about how wrong it was to be sexually involved in such activities with another boy. He gave me a very heavy penance and admonished me that it was a mortal sin that could send me to hell if I died before confessing it. I shook all over as he spoke those words and nearly fainted. Today it is a total blur in my mind. That was the first and only traumatic experience I had in the Catholic Church, but the guilt lasted well over a year.

In high school I knew I was gay and so did everyone else. I experienced the usual taunting and bullying that have psychologically harmed so many gay boys. But early in the second year of high school one boy made the mistake of harassing me when his friends weren't there to gang up on me, and I beat him up fairly badly. From that time on everyone left me alone.

I couldn't really talk openly with anyone about my sexual feelings, but became friends with other gay misfits in the school, though I never had sexual relations with any of them. To be honest, I sometimes fantasized about tying them up, whipping them, and having sex with them. But I had no sexual experiences with anyone until I went into the military shortly after I graduated, partly because of the lingering trauma from my parents' and the Irish priest's reactions to my play with Barry.

I was a loner and loved going to the library. I voraciously read everything I could find about homosexuality. Most of the clinical books only increased my fear that homosexuality was a perversion that would make my life miserable. Reading about the famous British playwright, Oscar Wilde, frightened me the most. I admired his adventurous freedom and defiance of social convention, but his experiences in prison terrified me. These negative portrayals of homosexuality were counterbalanced when I read novels by Mary Renault and Gore Vidal. Renault's novel, *The Last of the Wine*, about homosexuality in ancient Greece at the time of Socrates and Plato, was particularly uplifting as it normalized homosexuality as a part of human nature. Gore Vidal's novel, *The City and the Pillar*, has become quite controversial, but it introduced me to a wide variety of homosexual experiences in a mostly positive way — at least Vidal presented them as legitimate parts of human sexual experience. Interestingly, I also began reading about the history of corporal punishment, which deepened my fascination with the whipping fetish, now linked to sexual pleasure in my mind. I spent many hours thinking about corporal punishment while reading Scott Cleaver's *Under the Lash: A History of Corporal Punishment in the British Armed Forces*. William Cooper's *The History of the Rod* about flagellation throughout history also excited my imagination.

Overall, I had a positive experience with the Marist Brothers who ran St. Agnes Catholic High School, because they treated me with respect. Today, of course, we know that pedophilia was widespread in the Catholic Church at the time I was in high school. None of the brothers, however, ever made an advance on me, nor did I hear about it happening to anyone else. When I think back on how cute and attractive a few of the brothers were, I have fantasized about how much fun it would have been to have one of them initiate sexual play. That is, of course, only a fantasy; I know how harmful pedophile priests have been to vast numbers of gay and straight boys alike. Although there is no excuse for the actions of individual priests, the church and society in general should also take responsibility for creating and normalizing homophobia in the first place. Although I totally disavow the Catholic Church's stance on homosexuality and find nothing positive about the church's history of controlling sexuality in general, I remain thankful to the Marist Brothers who encouraged my intellectual and academic tendencies.

Seeing how much I enjoyed learning, the Marist Brothers encouraged me to consider a vocation to the priesthood. From one perspective, the idea of becoming a priest appealed to me. I loved to read and was an excellent student. I genuinely cared about people and have been drawn to spirituality and mysticism my whole life. I also knew that I could have a respected role in society without being stigmatized for my sexual orientation. From what I now know, the celibate priesthood was a way that many Catholic gay boys in those days tried to find a place in society. I, too, was tempted to escape the fate of Oscar Wilde by going into the priesthood.

In the 1960s boys most frequently entered the seminary upon graduation from high school. But some entered it during high school itself. Imagine that you are a boy between fourteen and eighteen years old and you enter the seminary. All sexuality is repressed just when most guys begin to experiment and learn about their own sexuality. In my opinion that's why there are so many alcoholic priests and why some become involved with young boys. The church, of course, created this environment by creating the climate of sexual repression in the first place. When the Church took young adolescents into the seminary, it created a powder keg. Sexual repression doesn't work and only creates a framework for abuse to happen.

Fear of social disgrace wasn't the only thing that drove my thoughts about becoming a priest. I have always been interested in spirituality and mysticism. I had been an altar boy for a while in my youth. About the same time that I first met Barry, I had borrowed altar boy vestments to take home; I would dress up, kneel down, and try to experience a union with God. The priest in the parish saw me bringing them back and asked me why I had taken them. I told him the truth, and he said that this was improper and he would have to relieve me from being an altar boy. Interestingly, the same priest was always personally supportive and even hired me for a short time to clean the church when I badly needed some money.

Although my father was very much against religion and went drinking on Sunday mornings, my mother was very religious and never missed Mass. My mother's uncle was a Jesuit priest who had been President of Fordham University. Because of my scholarly and spiritual interests, he was strongly pushing me to become a Jesuit. He got me a very good scholarship to Fordham. I knew, however, that the scholarship was really the first step to getting me into the priesthood. My self-enforced celibacy during high school, except occasionally masturbating to whipping fantasies, only increased my sexual desires and I could not imagine a life of denial and hiding. In our last discussion about this I remember looking him in the eye and telling him that I would not lead a life hiding and denying my homosexual desires. I told him I was firmly resolved to enlist in the Air Force. My great-uncle didn't speak to me for five years. Although I was talking about my personal decision, he undoubtedly felt that I was challenging his own decision to become a priest. I now know he was gay and had even attended the notorious gay sex parties of Cardinal Spellman. So he was one of those men who had chosen to lead a double life.

I could have been a good scholar and was very drawn to the mystical side of Catholic life. I still love history and reading about the past. I have never regretted my decision, but sometimes wistfully think about having had the life of a college professor. I remember my youthful attraction to some of the Catholic iconography of suffering saints, the flagellation of Jesus, and bound martyrs being tortured. I found both a spiritual and sexual release when I pictured myself being bound and whipped. Imaginatively, I felt a cathartic release and even a unity with the cosmos that I have subsequently found more viscerally in my sadomasochistic activities as a gay leatherman. This should not be so surprising or even shocking when one realizes that medieval mysticism glorified these same images and practices. Flagellation had been a part of Catholic mystical practices for centuries.

Early in my senior year in high school I realized that sublimating my sexual urges was too high a price to pay for social respectability. It has always been my instinct and my nature to confront controversial issues head on. I've never liked anyone telling me, even implicitly, that I didn't have any alternatives. The brothers in the Catholic high school had encouraged me to use my intellect to weigh social and moral issues. I reasoned that since my attraction to gay guys harmed no one, I shouldn't feel ashamed for the way God had created me. I never really believed that my play with Barry had been sinful. In fact, I felt quite positive about those experiences. Homosexuality as a great moral evil made no sense to me then and seems even more ludicrous today.

By the end of high school, I not only knew that there was nothing I could do about my attraction to men, there was nothing I wanted to do about it. So when I went into the military right out of high school, I left my Catholicism behind and totally discarded the Catholic Church's teachings on sexuality. My reading about the history of corporal punishment during high school often meant reading about men in the military throughout the ages. As a gay man I was drawn to living a life with other men, and the military seemed a more attractive way to live authentically than the priesthood. Neither the church nor its moral values were relevant in my life any longer.

Chapter 2: MILITARY

Iwas seventeen years old when I graduated from high school on June 25, 1962. Two days later I enlisted in the Air Force with my parents' permission. That's when I began to have a few sexual experiences with other men, although none of them involved any BDSM activity. After basic training, I was sent to the Air Force base in Biloxi, Mississippi, in September 1962, where I attended a technical school to learn the skills of Aircraft Control and Warning Radar. Andre Adams, who was from New Jersey, became my best friend. He was studying to become a radio operator and learning Morse code. From the very beginning, we really enjoyed each other's company. Although I suspected he might be gay, I didn't risk raising the issue. After we had known each other for a couple of weeks, however, he looked me in the eye and asked, "Are you sexually attracted to men?" I admitted that I was.

We cautiously began occasional sexual play. These were modern barracks with two men to a room. Occasionally, when one of our roommates was gone for a while and we were both off duty at the same time, we could fool around a little, playing with each other's dicks and sucking each other off. We would also sometimes shower together and soap each other up, alert to others coming into the john. If someone discovered us, he would most probably report us to the authorities, so we were very careful; that made the forbidden activities more exciting and also more dangerous, since in those days homosexuality was a cause for a dishonorable discharge from the military. I only remember one time, when most of the other recruits had taken a weekend pass to go into town, that Andre climbed into my bed for a short time. Though we didn't play sexually as often as I would have liked, we did become very good buddies and were often together.

Early on Andre and I went into a gay bar in Gulfport, my first. When we got back on base, we talked about how risky this had been, and we concluded that we wouldn't do it again. Someone who knew us might see us. Since I wasn't quite eighteen years old yet and looked even younger, I should not have been drinking in a bar and I feared that someone might ask to see my identification and report me to the officers back on the base. So that was the only time that I went into a gay bar in Mississippi.

Having grown up in New York City, I found Mississippi to be a real culture shock, very different from the romantic images in *Gone with the Wind*. In 1962 segregation in Mississippi was every bit as severe as apartheid in South Africa. Although the civil rights movement had begun to make progress in a few border states, government officials in the Deep South were defiant in the face of federal court rulings. At the Greyhound bus station in Biloxi, a white-only waiting room was air-conditioned with a cold-water drinking fountain and a white-only lunch counter. Blacks had to sit outside on hard benches in very hot, humid conditions. They had to drink out of hoses with warm water that tasted of rubber. If they wanted to order food from the lunch counter, they used an outside window. Most African-Americans were too poor to buy food and brought their lunches with them. I knew that in late 1960, the Supreme Court had ruled in *Boynton v. Virginia* that interstate commerce made it illegal to segregate lunch counters and waiting rooms in bus stations where passengers could take buses that crossed state lines. In Mississippi and Alabama, however, no one paid any attention to Supreme Court decisions or Federal court orders that required integration. Segregation was absolute, and racial tensions were at fever pitch. Governors Ross Barnett and George Wallace were increasing their electoral popularity by defying federal authorities.

The very month I arrived in Biloxi, Governor Barnett was standing in the doorway of the University of Mississippi to stop James Meredith, a young black man, from registering for classes, even though the federal courts had unanimously ruled in his favor. A couple of weeks after I arrived at the Air Force base, federal troops physically escorted Meredith into the building and forced the registrar to obey the law. The local radio station in Biloxi, WLOX, called itself "Radio Free Mississippi," and news broadcasters hysterically talked about the "invasion of Northern troops into the South."

So neither Andre, who was an African-American, nor I felt safe in downtown Biloxi. Interracial friendship was even more suspect. If we had not been wearing our Air Force uniforms, we would probably have been arrested on some trumped-up charge the first time we walked down the street together. One time we went to Gulfport to see *Whatever Happened to Baby Jane*, a psychological thriller starring Jane Crawford and Bette Davis, who were not only rivals in the film, but rivals in real life. I was seated downstairs in the orchestra for whites only and he had to go sit in the balcony. As soon as it got dark and the movie started, I sneaked up to the balcony to sit next to him. I was, of course, taking a risk in such a racially-charged climate.

Although the military was integrated and there was no problem with Andre and me being good friends on the base, we both realized very quickly that we were not safe riding local buses or even walking down the street together. Our fear of being arrested was very real, and we became even more concerned as racism became more virulent when the civil rights movement intensified in other parts of the South. On one early occasion

Andre and I got on a local bus together. He took a seat near the back of the bus, and without much reflection I followed and sat down beside him. The bus driver turned around and told me to get up front or get off the bus. Both Andre and I got off. We could not rely on the military to help us if we were arrested. The officers, in fact, told us that if we were arrested for violating the local segregation laws, the Air Force would charge us with being AWOL when we were released from jail. I still remember the chilling tone of the sergeant when he said, "You will respect the local customs."

Experiencing segregation in Mississippi made me grow up pretty quickly. I was no longer a boy, but became a man, suddenly aware of social injustice and human cruelty. My terror of being arrested with Andre was matched only by my defiant personality. I knew that violating the social mores in Mississippi would not be treated like a boyhood prank, but I seethed inside that people thought they could dictate my friendships. I was a seventeen-year-old airman whose best friend was black, and as gay men we were even more isolated. My friendship with Andre was one of the deepest friendships of my life.

In December 1962 both Andre and I were reassigned — he to a base in Texas and I to the Sioux City Air Force Base in Iowa. Although I missed him, I was relieved to be out of the Deep South. I was wearing the Air Force uniform when I arrived, but almost no one believed that I was actually a recruit. The guys even bet on whether it was my father's or brother's uniform. The few who bet that I was actually a recruit probably won quite a bit of small change. I was five foot three inches, weighed 120 pounds, and had a twenty-seven-inch waist; I must have looked like a fourteen or fifteen-year old.

Sometime in early 1963 I was hitchhiking and was picked up by a very good-looking man in his thirties who lived alone in Omaha. I had by then turned eighteen years old. Driving down the road he nonchalantly put his hand on my upper thigh, and I moved a little closer to him. We both obviously wanted the same thing, and he suggested that I go home with him. For the next few months we saw each other regularly – I took weekend leaves and visited him. And we were even able to arrange a couple of vacations together. We had strictly vanilla gay sex together – hugging, massaging, frottage, and oral sex. In the privacy of his home, for the first time in my life, I didn't have to fear discovery. Without any question, I now accepted myself as a gay man and felt no guilt or shame. A few months later we drifted apart.

In the early summer of 1963, my sergeant, "Woody" Woodward asked whether I would be interested in mowing his lawn. I learned later that his wife had taken their two daughters back to her parents' house after a series of domestic squabbles. On one particularly hot, humid July day, when I had finished mowing his lawn, he said that he had drawn a cool bath in the tub for me. I didn't hesitate and went inside the house and climbed in the bathtub. I was relaxing when he came in stark naked. "Woody" was a great nickname for him – his cock was rock hard, and mine became equally hard almost immediately. He climbed into the tub, took me into his arms, and then got into the "69" position where we both had access to each other's cocks, and we began kissing and sucking each other. We were both so excited that we ejaculated almost immediately. As soon as we dried off, we both got hard-ons again. He took me into the bedroom, and I still remember his licking my balls and cock. It was quite late when I left his house, and I hoped that he would want to see me again. I didn't have to fear that. His lawn now seemed to need mowing almost every weekend, and we continued the affair for several months. I spent many weekends with him, often returning to the base in his car early on Monday mornings.

Sometime in late October the commanding officers learned that an obviously homosexual airman was having sex with lots of guys on the base. They confronted him, and he admitted it immediately. When they asked him the names of the guys he had sex with, he implicated about eighty others. On a base of 900 men, that was nearly 10 percent of the guys. I had not had sex with him and therefore was not implicated, but Sergeant Woodward was named. Then I noticed that guys began to disappear from the base. Just when everything seemed resolved and I could breathe a sigh of relief, someone sent a letter to the commander of the base about his suspicions that I was having a sexual affair with Sergeant Woodward. He had apparently seen us returning to the base in Woody's car early on Monday mornings.

The officer from the Office of Special Investigations called us into his office separately. I don't know what Woody told the officer, but I decided to tell the truth about the beginning of our relationship: Sergeant Woodward had invited me in to take a cool bath and then came into the room naked and climbed in the bathtub with me. I suspect that Woody told them that I had seduced him, because he was allowed to remain in the military, and he apparently pleaded with his wife to come back with their two daughters, because they returned shortly afterward.

On December 20, 1963, I was given a general discharge under honorable conditions. The papers said that it was for "inadaptability to service life," and also "an act of sexual perversion." I suspect that the Commander knew that I had been telling the truth, so he did not give me a dishonorable discharge as most of the other men had received. Sergeant Woodward had probably served so long that the commander wanted to give him a second chance, especially now that his wife had returned. I had truthfully said that my sergeant had initiated the sexual activity. I did not, however, admit I was a homosexual. I'm not proud of lying, but I was not going to be foolish. My general discharge under honorable conditions allowed me to get veterans' benefits that have been very important to me in my later life. I later also used the GI Bill to get a degree from San Francisco Community College.

I'll never forget the kindness or the words of the Commander when we had the exit interview in his office. "You are deeply hurt now by this, but in a few months it won't seem like such a tragedy. You'll go on with your life. And a few months later, you'll have no regrets, but you'll remember the good times you've had in the Air Force." He reached out to shake my hand and said, "Thank you very much for your service. Have a good life." I have always been grateful to him not only for his kind words, but even more that he did not give me a dishonorable discharge, allowing me to have access to veterans' benefits for all these years.

Chapter 3: YOUNG LEATHERMAN IN NEW YORK

I returned to New York just before Christmas in 1963. My parents were then living in a small cottage on an estate in New Jersey, not too far from New York City, where my Mother was the cook and my Dad the chauffeur. They welcomed me to stay with them, though I hoped to get my own place in the City when I could afford it. When my parents asked about my discharge from the Air Force, I told them part of the truth — that I had received a "general discharge under honorable conditions" because of "inadaptability to service life." I didn't mention, however, that it was also for "an act of sexual perversion."

In a few weeks, thanks to help from a friend of the family, I got an entry-level job as a financial analyst at Merrill Lynch. My parents' cottage was too small for more than a short stay, so I got a room in a brownstone that had been cut up into about ten small apartments — mine had a bathroom and kitchenette. It was close to the Brooklyn Bridge, so I was able to walk across it to work every day, since my brokerage office was just on the other side. Excitedly, I began to explore gay life in the city. Since I could legally drink at age eighteen in New York, I frequented a few gay bars and occasionally went home with someone, though I really didn't form any close relationships or even friendships. Those were the days when the police vice squad would raid a gay bar and shut it down, so I didn't get to know any of the guys very well. During these early months, I heard about The Empire Theater on 42nd Street, where men would go to have sex with other guys.

The theater had been quite elegant when built in 1912. Thomas Lamb, a noted architect, had designed it, and many prominent stage plays had opened there. By the 1960s, however, it had become a bit seedy, and second-rate movies played all day long and late into the evening. Lots of unemployed and homeless people would go into the theatre to escape the summer heat and the winter cold. Tickets were only fifty cents before noon. Homeless men would stay on the ground floor, sleeping in the theater seats, while gay guys went up to the balconies to have sex.

On Easter Sunday 1964, three months after I returned from the Air Force, I bought my first theater ticket and went in to check the place out. After climbing to the first balcony, I stood off to one side. When my eyes adjusted to the dimness, I saw that some guys were jerking off under their coats, and other guys were in darker areas obviously sucking cock. My heart pounded with excitement, not knowing what would happen. Almost immediately a guy in his thirties sidled up close to me, looking into my eyes. I liked his looks and stared back at him. He took a step closer and fingered his fly. I was there for sex, so I impulsively knelt as he got closer, putting my face near his crotch, while he unzipped his pants. That was the first of many cocks that I sucked in the Empire Theatre.

When he finished and moved off, I took a seat so I could survey the whole balcony. To my astonishment, I heard slapping sounds coming from the second balcony above us that could only come from ass beating. I instantly thought of spanking Barry years earlier, and my cock got rock hard as I excitedly climbed to the second balcony. I had never imagined that older men were actually into whipping and spanking as a sexual activity; I had thought of it as play activity between kids like Barry and me. When I reached the second balcony, I stood in the shadows in a daze. Not only were the shadowy figures paddling and strapping one another, but many of them were also wearing boots and leather jackets. In a back corner one particularly tall, muscular guy was beating another guy's ass with a thick leather belt. The bottom was on all fours, his pants down to his ankles, his ass up in the air, groaning as the Top swung the doubled-up belt. Instinctively I got down on all fours, crawled over to them, and began licking the tall man's leather boots. He stopped swinging his belt and pressed his hand on the back of my neck, pushing my face down even more onto his boots. After a few moments he moved me alongside the other sub and told me to pull my pants down to my ankles. Then he began swinging the doubled-up belt again, this time aiming for both my ass and that of the guy next to me. That was my first real experience as a leatherman.

  I didn't go home with anyone that Easter Sunday, but I did a few days later. When I went to the Empire Theatre after that, I often ended up spending the weekend at some guy's place. I wasn't too particular about the men I accompanied home, but I enjoyed exploring gay sex with occasional bondage and some impact play, mostly ass beating. I don't remember ever getting together with the same guy more than once, but I was not looking for anything more than hook-ups and casual play.

  I had been cruising the second floor balcony at the Empire Theatre for a few months when, in late May, I saw a very muscular, blond guy looking at me. He was wearing a dark shirt, a black leather motorcycle jacket with a belt around the waist, and black leather pants. When he continued to stare at me, I stared back, inviting him to approach. He was about six foot four inches tall and in his early thirties. He grabbed my head and roughly pushed me down on his boots. I dutifully started licking them. I was as sexually excited as I had ever been at the Empire Theatre. He bent down and whispered in my ear, "Do you want to go home with me?" I was in a dream. Here was my fantasy image of a leatherman, and he wanted me to go home with him! Without any hesitation, I nodded my head and said, "Yes, Sir." He gently pulled me to my feet, and we walked down the stairs and out of the building. He introduced himself as David and told me that his apartment was in Hell's Kitchen.

When we arrived, he gently pushed me through the door, his hand on the back of my neck. There was no more small talk or conversation of any kind. He ordered me into his bedroom and told me to strip. Although I wasted no time, he seemed dissatisfied that I wasn't getting undressed faster. Although his abruptness and sudden change of personality made me a little uneasy, I was excited by it and hurried to comply with his orders. "Turn around and face the wall."

He told me to open my mouth and then shoved a gag into me. I must have seemed to be resisting, because he immediately barked, "You will learn to obey me." Fear competed with sexual excitement. Everything occurred so quickly that I really had no time to think about anything that was happening. I could only react. From the moment I saw him in the Empire Theatre balcony, I had mentally played a submissive role. I expected him to be Dominant and interpreted his actions as sexual role-play. Before I could react to the gag, he tied my hands behind my back and put a blindfold on me. Even when he threw me over the bed and secured me to it with ropes, I remained sexually excited.

Without any warm-up, he hit me hard on the ass with a quirt and then continued to strike me as hard and fast as he could on my back, legs, and ass. Then my excitement suddenly changed to fright. What earlier seemed like Dominance disclosed itself as sheer brutality. His aggression matched my building terror. I tried to scream, "Stop" through the gag. The more I yelled, the more excited he got, and the harder he hit me. After a few minutes I realized that the more I struggled and screamed, the more excited and vicious he became. I tried as much as I could to push aside my dread and ignore the pain. I feared that he was some kind of serial killer who would murder me.

Despite the terror, I fortunately had the presence of mind to realize that my shrieks were only exciting him more. I went limp and used every stoic ounce of energy I had to remain still. That seemed to piss him off even more. He threw the whip down, slapped me a few times, and brutally raped me. There was nothing I could do to stop him; I only hoped that he wouldn't kill me. He had his orgasm. Needless to say my dick was totally limp. When he unshackled me, I wondered how I could escape from his apartment. "You're the worst fuck I've ever had, you miserable faggot. Get the fuck out of my apartment." He opened the door, pushed me out, and threw my clothes at me. I wasted no time getting out of there. As I ran down the street, I kept looking over my shoulder, fearing he was following me.

I don't remember how or when I got dressed or even my leaving the apartment house. A few blocks away, I remember collapsing against a lamppost, out-of-breath, and shaking uncontrollably. I immediately began blaming myself: "How could I have been so stupid?" "What had I done to cause him to brutalize and rape me?" I eventually made it back to my apartment. I had no one to tell. I couldn't go to the police, because I had gone with him freely. Since gay sex was a crime, I had willingly participated in a crime. I wasn't even sure I wanted to tell anyone how stupid I had been. I was enraged, however, by this asshole who had brutalized me, but I was equally angry with myself for being such a fool. Years later, of course, I now realize that I was the victim and was not responsible for being raped.

For several weeks I had no desire for sex of any kind, and I had no desire to return to the Empire Theatre. I became apprehensive about the BDSM activities that took place there because of their association in my mind with the ferocious rape. For the next couple of months my dread of getting harmed or even killed eclipsed any joy in getting my ass whipped by a hot man in leather. My sexual desire did, of course, begin to return in full force after three or four weeks. At first, I didn't want to go back to the Empire Theatre, because of its association with my scary experience.

I had earlier cruised Bryant Park for sex. Cruising for anonymous sex is not just about the physical act of getting or giving a blowjob. There is an excitement similar to that of a fisherman wondering whether a fish would take his lure. The men in the park were both hunters and prey. Was I cute enough to attract some hot guy? Should I return the stare that someone else gave me? Public, or quasi-public, sex has always excited me and many other gay men. The danger of getting caught aroused me. Shadowy forms emerged from the bushes as I got closer to them. My heart pounded when I saw one of the dark figures approaching. Some guys in Bryant Park were wearing leather jackets and boots, and I thrilled when those men desired me. When my eyes connected with a handsome man in leather, he would become my leather god, and I would hold his gaze, getting down on my knees. He would approach, standing before me, whip out his cock, and expect me to take it into my mouth. The anonymity of the night, the rustling of the wind in the trees, the ripened smell of a man's erection, my trembling body — all put me into a state of euphoria. My senses were totally alive, and the distractions of everyday life disappeared. In my mind the cock I was servicing became the cocks of all men throughout time. It became the cosmic phallus worthy of worship. Taking it into my mouth was like taking Holy Communion, more sacred than anything I had experienced in the Catholic Church. Becoming sexual again in Bryant Park facilitated my recovery, but I still didn't dare to go home with anyone, at least not yet.

Picking up a hustler is an activity like cruising. Both are anonymous, exciting, and mysterious. One hot, humid day in July at Coney Island later that summer I met an attractive guy who was hustling. When he approached me, I wasn't really looking for sex, but couldn't resist his dark hair and blue eyes. After I told him that I didn't have much money, he said, "I sometimes don't charge when I find someone who I'd enjoy being with." His name was David, and he was only a couple of years older than I was. I never learned his last name or anything about his past. He continued hustling, but I visited him during the weekends. He was my first on-going relationship with a guy my own age, and I imagined myself being in love and living a more regular life as a gay man. I felt special, because David never wanted me to pay for sex, though he charged everyone else. He was a good lover, and I even fantasized that I might become his domestic partner. David, however, had no desire for any kind of permanent relationship. When he realized that I was falling in love with him, he gently ended the relationship. David was a very thoughtful lover, and my time with him over a six-week period further helped me push aside the brutal rape.

In late summer when my brief relationship with David ended, I got up my nerve to go back to the Empire Theatre. I decided that I would not go home with anyone, but could enjoy the ass beating, cock sucking, and bootlicking that took place in the second balcony. When I ventured back to the theatre, I saw a black guy in leather sucking another guy's cock. When I took a closer look, I recognized my good friend Andre from the Air Force. I was surprised that he was wearing leather and obviously interested in leathersex. There had been no hint of BDSM or even Top/bottom play when we had fooled around on the Air Force base. Standing in the shadows, I watched Andre finish sucking off a man wearing a leather jacket and leather boots. When he stood up I walked up behind him, lowered my voice, and asked, "Are you going to beat my ass or am I going to give you the whipping you deserve?" Startled, he turned around. When he saw me, he was speechless and immediately followed me out of the theatre into the street where we talked for hours about everything that had happened to us. I learned that he, too, had been discharged from the Air Force after getting caught up in a sexual incident with another guy. We learned that we had similar interests in BDSM. I ended up going home with him in the Bronx, where he was living with two other guys. I even told him about the rape, and over the next couple of months he helped me gain the courage to explore the leather world in New York City more aggressively. Although Andre and I were not monogamous lovers, we were great friends and liked being with each other. We eventually lived together for more than four years in New York and San Francisco.

A couple of months after moving in with Andre, I saw the famous *Life* magazine issue, published in June 1964, about a new kind of homosexual that defied the then current stereotype that gay guys were effeminate. The lead article was entitled "Homosexuality in America," with a caption that read, "A Secret World Grows Open and Bolder." Although the articles in the magazine presented the dominant psychiatric view that homosexuality was a mental disorder, astonishingly they also presented opposing views. One article, for example, quoted psychologist Evelyn Hooker, an early gay activist who asserted that same sex relationships existed among many animal species and therefore was a "natural" deviation from the heterosexual norm. She also pointed out that gay men and lesbians who sought out psychologists did so because they were not coping well with life for a variety of reasons. They were not, she argued, representative of the vast majority of homosexuals, any more than heterosexuals in therapy were the norm for all straight men and women.

The article in *Life* opened with a two-page photo spread of butch guys in leather jackets and boots, standing in front of Chuck Arnett's famous mural of masculine gay men. The photo was taken in the Tool Box, the earliest leather bar in the South of Market district of San Francisco. The caption under the picture read, "A San Francisco bar run by homosexuals is crowded with patrons who wear leather jackets, make a show of masculinity and scorn effeminate members of their world." Gay guys, the writer stressed, arrived at this bar on motorcycles. The article quoted Bill Ruquy, one of the owners of the bar: "This is a place for men, a place without all those screaming faggots, fuzzy sweaters and sneakers." Even though there were symbols of hyper-masculinity all around and "everything looks tough," Ruquy also claimed that the Tool Box was "probably the most genteel bar in town." I couldn't stop staring at the picture of these men in leather, some wearing motorcycle caps, denoting their Dominance. I never found the early leather scene in New York at this time, let alone one where gay men rode motorcycles. I wanted to be part of this scene and knew that I needed to move to San Francisco as soon as possible. My excitement was contagious, and Andre decided he would go out West with me.

My enthusiasm even affected my parents, who thought that it would be wonderful to work in the temperate climate of California. My father had tired of shoveling snow on the estate in New Jersey that winter, and my mother thought they could easily find work in a rich suburb south of San Francisco. Although I couldn't officially ask to be transferred to the San

Francisco offices of Merrill Lynch, I learned that with my experience I would easily get hired there if I just showed up. So in the spring of 1966 my parents and I loaded up their car, and we drove across the country. Since Andre didn't have a job waiting for him in San Francisco, we decided that he would join me later. I started working full time at Merrill Lynch only a few days after arriving in San Francisco. I moved into an apartment in the Haight District on Carl Street, very near Maude's, an early San Francisco lesbian bar, was around the corner. My parents temporarily moved in with me, but within a couple of weeks found positions on an estate in Atherton, just down the peninsula from San Francisco.

Chapter 4: YOUNG LEATHERMAN IN SAN FRANCISCO

When I arrived in San Francisco in the spring of 1966, I was still only twenty years old, and I looked even younger. When I tried to sneak into the Tool Box, the doorman told me to come back in a few years when I was "of age." Instead, I came back a couple of months later on June 16, my twenty-first birthday, with a valid ID. I still have vivid memories of walking into the leather bar made iconic by *Life* magazine. I was wearing leather boots, jeans, and a white T-shirt. The masculine energy in the bar created an electric atmosphere. My heart beat in rhythm with the pounding beat of loud country and western music. Guys dressed in black leather and boots jostled past each other, their sweaty aromas mixing with beer and tobacco. The sight of men in their leathers, along with the smells and deafening sound of music, created an unforgettable erotic atmosphere, a sensory overload. I was "new meat," young, boyish, and cute. A bit of an exhibitionist, I relished the attention of the Dominant, masculine men who watched me enter the bar that first time. I was in my element. Most early leather bars had dimly lit back rooms with plenty of groping, oral sex, and, very occasionally, even fucking. My experiences in the Empire Theater in New York gave me the confidence to throw myself into these sexual activities, and I became quite popular.

In these early days there wasn't a lot of flexibility about roles, at least publicly. If you were a Top you wore your keys on the left side, or you wore a chain on the left shoulder of your leather jacket, or on your left boot. If you were a bottom you wore them on the right. (At that same period, the codes were reversed on the East Coast, and that has led to some confusion.) Although some guys switched from bottom to Top after they had been in the scene for a while, they generally only switched once. In truth, there were some perceived Tops who would occasionally bottom for someone in private, though they never admitted it publicly. No one would wear chains on both sides when they were in a leather bar in those days; I never heard anyone use the word "switch."

The Why Not? in the Tenderloin district had actually been the first leather bar in San Francisco and featured the famous Tony Tavarossi logo, but it had closed by the time I got to the city. Although the Tool Box was the bar for leather men on bikes when I turned twenty-one, Febe's opened soon after on Folsom Street and quickly surpassed the Tool Box in popularity. Motorcycles lined the street in front of it for more than a block on Saturday nights. The Taste of Leather, a leather and sex-toy shop upstairs, owned and run by Nick O'Demus, added to its popularity. Artist Mike Caffee created and displayed his original *Leather David* as a centerpiece and logo of the bar. It became extremely popular in leather circles and was reproduced by the hundreds, many finding homes in other leather bars throughout the United States and even in Europe. The Stud, nearby on Folsom Street, opened about the same time. By the summer of 1968 there were at least a half-dozen bars on the strip that became known as "The Miracle Mile." A year or so later there were at least ten leather bars and baths in the South of Market area.

If you were in a gay bar on a Friday or Saturday night when they announced "last call" and didn't have a date, there was always a private party somewhere. The bartender knew where the party was and helped spread the word. You could get into these parties with either a six-pack, which the bartender would sell you for a couple of bucks, or you could pay three dollars at the door. Most guys brought beer.

These were sex parties — really orgies — with 100 to 150 guys. There wasn't much leather or BDSM play at them in the first years that I was in San Francisco. Three or four years later, however, as the leather scene grew, the after-hours parties increasingly included Dominance and submission with activities such as bootlicking. I remember one party in the early 1970s on the twenty-ninth floor of the Fox Plaza on Market Street in the Civic Center. Over one hundred guys, stuffed into a three-bedroom apartment, were sucking cock or fucking. A few guys engaged in light leather play that emphasized Dominance and submission. About an hour and a half into the party everyone was pretty drunk, and some guys dropped beer cans off the balcony. Of course, the cops came and the party was over. That happened on several occasions, but usually the parties went on until 5:00 or 6:00 a.m. Everyone got all the sex they wanted at these late night parties — this was San Francisco in the late 60s and early 70s before the AIDS epidemic.

Quite often, however, I would hook up with a guy and go to his place after cruising the leather bars Friday or Saturday night. At first, I didn't discriminate much when a good-looking guy wanted to take me home. I sucked a lot of cock and occasionally got fucked. I got what I was looking for — and lots of it! After a while it became clear that I had no trouble attracting play dates. I was the cute young boy, tough enough to take whatever a Top was dishing out. Soon I realized that I could become more selective. I carefully observed how Tops and bottoms hooked up. A shy Top might appreciate it when a bottom took the initiative and flirted with him, but generally the most popular Tops wanted to believe they did the choosing. They would spurn any bottom who began openly flirting with them. There were, of course, subtle ways for a bottom to take some initiative. I learned to stand close to a guy who interested me, look at him until I saw him glance at me, and then avert my eyes. Dominance and submission were a ritualistic game that began in the leather bars and then extended into private play space.

After signaling that I was interested in a particular Top in the leather bar, I would distance myself and casually chat with guys whom I'd met before. If another Top tentatively invited me to go home with him, I would tell him something ambiguous: "I'm just hanging out for now." Through these subtle rituals, Tops knew whether or not a bottom was seriously interested in going home with them, even before they made a direct offer. Yet these rituals also preserved the powerful sexual dynamic of Dominance and submission. As the evening got later and guys began drifting off together, I would cease circulating among friends and excuse myself to take a piss or get a last beer. I would then stand alone near the Top who had interested me. If he was interested, he might motion me to come join his group or, if he was ready to leave, he would look at me inquisitively, and I would nod or perhaps stare at his boots, and he would know that I'd go home with him. If he didn't signal, then I would know he had something else in mind and would continue cruising elsewhere. A few popular Tops could have the pick of any bottom in the bar, so it was always a gamble. As I played this game more and more, I became better at it. I always found it exciting.

There was a real community in the leather bars in the late 1960s and early 70s. You could tell whether someone was respected by the way the other men related to him. Tops and bottoms both earned their reputations through their expertise, interactions with others, and the quality of their play. As a bottom, I could tell a lot about a Top's reputation by the way he interacted with other Tops. When a Top was respected, other Tops would enjoy being in his company, and there would be laughter and easy conversation. If a Top wasn't respected, then he would be isolated and ignored by others. In a few cases, word would spread to avoid some guy who had not respected his partner's limits; then it would be difficult for him to find future partners. If a guy was truly dangerous and had injured someone, then the Tops would take direct action to make sure that he did not injure anyone else. If a bottom was uncertain about someone, he could always ask the bartender, who would convey information not only by what he said, but also by his stance and how he answered the question. When I once asked the bartender about someone, he simply shrugged and looked me in the eye as if to say, "I can't be certain, but I'd be careful before I went home with him." In all the time I was cruising Tops in a leather bar, I never went home with anyone who presented any danger. The community of leathermen provided safety.

While I had dates with lots of guys, there were three Tops who became special to me in those first six months that I was in San Francisco: Thom Gunn, Bill Bliss, and Billy Lytton. The first two were well established in the leather community and more than fifteen years older than I was. They were very popular Tops who could have the pick of any bottom in the bar. Billy was only a couple of years older, and we explored the world of leather together.

When Thom Gunn walked into the bar, conversation stopped and guys took notice. He was tall, handsome, and impeccably dressed in leather. I stared at him as he handed his motorcycle helmet to the barkeeper, who hung it on the wall. The bartender automatically brought him a beer; he was clearly a regular. A sense of command and authority surrounded him, and he was part of a group of Tops who enjoyed each other's company. I felt his sexual energy. He looked around the bar and I instinctively knew that he could have almost any bottom in the bar. Instantly, I fantasized about going home with him, but I knew my chances were slim to non-existent, as he barely looked at me. I was staring at him longer than I should, and I averted my eyes with difficulty. All evening I surreptitiously watched him move about the bar talking with friends. After the first initial glance, I never saw him look at me again. A couple of hours later, however, he was suddenly standing next to me and smiled. "I'm going home now, so follow me if you want." Before I could even respond, he was at the bar, getting his helmet from the bartender. He walked out the door without glancing in my direction, but I dutifully followed him to his motorcycle. He handed me a spare helmet, and I climbed on behind him and put my arms around his waist. With the motorcycle throbbing beneath us we sped across the Bay Bridge to Berkeley as the intoxicating smell of leather enhanced the salty fog of the cool summer air.

I didn't know anything about him when he first picked me up at the Tool Box. Later I found out that he was a professor at UC Berkeley, and an internationally-known poet from England, who had written many collections of poems. He became openly gay after immigrating to the United States and began to include his gay experiences in his poetry. Although he was at the beginning of his career when I met him, he would later receive many literary prizes and eventually a MacArthur Award for Excellence. Perhaps his most famous work, written in 1992, was "The Man with Night Sweats," that described his grief for many lost friends during the AIDS crisis of the 1980s.

But I didn't go home with Thom in 1966 because of his literary fame; I went home with him because he was extremely sexy, and everything about him exuded a confident masculinity. He took command naturally without theatrics, and I learned that first night that he was a terrific leather Top. I've often been asked what makes a man a great leather Top. The answer is actually the same for both Tops and bottoms. Great players put a lot of energy into creating a good scene that is mutually satisfying and creates a strong masculine bonding. Both have to be honest about their experience levels, limitations, and desires. Both Tops and bottoms have to respect each other and themselves. Both have to be adventurous and willing to try new activities. And, of course, the Top has to know what he is doing — both technically and psychologically.

Thom Gunn was both technically proficient and knew how to create a thrilling and sexy scene. From the moment that he looked at me, smiled, and said, "I'm going home now, so follow me if you want," he was self-assured, yet gentle. I instinctively knew he would be caring, and I wanted to entrust myself to him. When we got to his place, he smiled at me and held the door open. I accepted his offer of a beer, and he motioned me to sit down at the table while he went into the bathroom. I glanced around his kitchen. Though uncluttered, it was clearly used. I relaxed and sipped the beer. A few minutes later he came back and sat down across from me. Looking at me with a friendly smile, he immediately put me at ease. He asked me about my experience with leather play, and I briefly told him about my experiences in New York City at the Empire Theatre and about playing here in San Francisco.

After a few minutes, he said, "I think you'll be fun to play with." I smiled, realizing that it was time for our play to begin. He stood up, put his hands on my shoulders, and gently pushed me toward his bedroom. He told me to strip and pulled off his belt. He put one arm around me, bent me slightly over, and began whipping my ass. He started slowly, each blow precisely aimed. He clearly knew what he was doing, and I felt completely safe and even protected as I felt the blows. Eventually he pushed me down over the edge of his bed. I wanted to serve him and give him pleasure, because he made me feel special, both in the way he touched me and by the carefully chosen words telling me how much he enjoyed making my cute ass red. His pacing was perfect, always keeping me excited and on edge, while pushing me to accept ever more pain without overwhelming me. When he gave me an especially hard swat, he would wait until I relaxed again to give me the next one. I was with a Top who had good technique and knew what he was doing, so I could relax and follow the rhythm.

Thom would swing the belt and I would react. He would adjust his own next move depending on my reactions. What made him such a great Top? He led me in a wonderfully fulfilling sexual dance and paid attention to my reactions and took them into account as he beat my ass. What makes a bottom a good bottom? While following Thom's lead, I allowed myself to react in body movements and tone of voice in saying, "Thank you Sir," thus signaling my honest reactions to the pain he was giving me. That night Thom and I relished our dance of Domination and submission, giving and accepting the erotic pain that carried both of us into ecstasy. All good scenes require honest communication and good connection, most of it accomplished through a body language that one learns through practice.

Thom circled his hand around my hard dick as he gave my ass another blow with the belt. With my dick dripping with excitement and my ass pleasantly burning, my only thoughts were about pleasing him and hoping he was enjoying himself. When his blows became stronger, I welcomed them as a sign of his own sexual excitement. And the blows were exciting me as well. When he pushed me down on my knees and whipped out his rock hard, ample cock, I wanted to taste it, excited at the thought of giving him pleasure. After he had cum, he removed the rest of his clothes and took me to bed with him. He was a considerate Top and wanted me to get off as well. He played with my cock, and it wasn't long before I reached orgasm. Lying in his arms, we dozed, but woke up to play several times more in the night. I felt totally fulfilled as he used my holes for his pleasure, and my own orgasms were an icing on the cake. In the morning he fixed a light breakfast for us and then took me back to San Francisco on his bike.

I played with Thom at his home perhaps a half dozen times a year over a seven-year period, first in Berkeley and then in Mill Valley in Marin County. When he died I bought his belt at an auction for charity, and it is one of the most precious items I own. Thom kept the sex exciting; I never knew quite what to expect. Although he was reliably safe, he was quite adventurous. One warm evening he took me out into the woods and strung me up to a tree, whipped me, and then put me over a log to fuck me. Other times he would be more relaxed at home, but would suddenly take charge after lulling me into thinking we would spend the night cuddling. Although I knew that I would usually have my back whipped or my butt paddled, I never knew how or when it would happen. That kept the sex exciting.

I had moved to San Francisco because I found the gay men who dressed in leather and rode motorcycles very sexy and wanted to be a part of that scene. I loved being among all the hot guys in leather. Many were ex-military and loved wearing uniforms. They wore their leather boots, jackets, belts, and harnesses with pride in their gay masculinity. They called each other "Sir" and ranked themselves informally on their skills and experience. They wore their keys on the left and usually sported motorcycle caps. Both Tops and bottoms followed a military code of ethics that included honesty and honor that kept everyone safe, even when masculine sex play became quite rough. As a young new guy in the leather scene and very much a submissive bottom at that point in my life, I was deferential to them. To be honest, I was primarily looking for a Top to fuck me and I was looking to ride with a hot guy on a motorcycle. And I loved sucking cock and giving pleasure to another man.

As a bottom I waited for Thom and other Tops to take the lead in our leather play, and I understood that these men would enjoy me and take pleasure in using me. And the Tops knew that bottoms got sexual pleasure from serving them and being used. Except for a few rather selfish Tops, they also wanted to give their bottoms a good time and sexual enjoyment as well. If they had not, they would have fewer and fewer bottoms who would want to play with them.

The leather world in those days was very much divided into Tops and bottoms. Both knew their roles in these sexual play scenes. Most guys thought that Dominants and submissives were born that way. Codes of behavior enhanced this division, both in the leather bars and in play scenes. Dominants were addressed as Sir, while submissives of any age were usually referred to as "boy." Dominants took charge and submissives responded. Tops wore their keys on the left, bottoms on the right. Bottoms waited for a Top to approach them and speak to them. Although for the most part leathermen observed these codes, everyone understood that play was about sexual enjoyment and cementing the close bonds between men.

A few very talented Tops, such as Thom Gunn, incorporated Dominance and submission into their sex play. This role play took place in the leather bars and subsequent sex scenes in their homes. Some men, however, carried their Dominance and submissiveness beyond sex into their general lives. A few of them came together as Masters and slaves, terms that took on a specific meaning within the leather community.

Although, in their eyes, it was not a matter of superiority or inferiority, the relationships were in fact hierarchical. In this worldview, Dominants were created to lead and submissives to follow. Then, as now, the Master/slave scene was a small, but very committed, part of the leather community. When I arrived in San Francisco there were a half-dozen well-known Master/slave families, where a Master lived with one or more slaves. A well-known family included Jim Kane, his slave Ike Barnes, and his protégé Guy Baldwin. Even for those of us who weren't interested in being slaves, these houses provided a sexy environment when we wanted sadomasochistic impact play.

After only a couple of months at the Tool Box, I became known as a serious s/m player who enjoyed and could take a lot of pain — a pain pig. I suppose that was the reason why Bill Bliss, the head of another prominent Master/slave house, became interested in me. In his forties, he was obviously well respected by other leathermen at the Tool Box. I felt honored by his attention and didn't hesitate going home with him whenever he invited me. When I went to his place, Bill would first establish the framework of Dominance and submission. He would tell me to strip and then kneel with my hands behind my back, eyes looking at the floor. I waited while he prepared something. Kneeling and waiting increased the sexual tension that was part of Bill's Master/slave play. I remember my heart thumping when he returned, took me downstairs, and tied me to the St. Andrew's Cross. He took his time choosing the whip, and my sexual tension increased. The first touch of his whip created an instant bond between us. Subsequent blows increased the tension further, until I was "flying." How long? When a bottom enters the zone, there is no time. Eventually some final blows of the whip relieve the tension. When the chemistry is right between a Top and bottom, there can be an emotional catharsis, a feeling of cleansing and relief. When I played with Bill, my ego faded away, and there was a spiritual connection between us. At that moment I felt my universe expand, and a feeling of love seemed to encompass all of reality.

Like everything in Bill's life, his play was meticulous. He was known in the leather community for being impeccably dressed in leather; he had outfits for every occasion. He owned an exclusive antique shop that specialized in expensive silver items. Every morning, like clockwork, he would walk to his store, wearing an expensive, well-tailored suit. His partner, Bill Meyer, wore a locked chain around his neck that marked him as his slave.

After Bill Bliss took me home to play, I became part of a circle of guys who occasionally surrounded him at the Tool Box. I naturally got invited to his next dungeon party, which always started with a formal dinner. These were wonderful affairs, great meals, and special occasions in the leather community, but we were not equal in any sense. Bill invited the most respected leathermen, mostly Doms, to sit at the head table. A few "slaves" had the privilege of formally serving food at the head table. Those who were chosen for this task found great satisfaction in serving the leather Masters. The slaves followed elaborate protocols about proper ways to serve, thereby gaining respect from everyone present. I think that Bill saw this training as part of the process where a bottom could aspire to be one of his part-time slaves.

Bill Bliss epitomized today's picture of an "Old Guard" Master. When you were in his house, you followed elaborate protocols, and his slaves followed even more elaborate household protocols. Everything about those meals emphasized a hierarchical distinction between Dominants and submissives. Those of us who were boys and subs, but not serving and preparing the meal, sat on the floor or at lesser tables. I often thought that Bill was trying to duplicate his memories of life in Paris, where he and his family fled from Czarist Russia after the Bolshevik revolution. Even after immigrating to the United States, he still maintained the high style of nobility in his home with fine china and beautifully upholstered chairs.

After we finished dinner, we would all play in Bill's formal dungeon that could have been in one of Larry Townsend's or John Preston's novels about gay Masters and slaves. In Bill Bliss's house everything was impeccably clean and neatly organized. There were bondage tables, Saint Andrew's Crosses, and cages. Whips, straps, and paddles were carefully hung on the walls. The lights were dim, and everything was painted dark. The play itself seemed to emphasize the hierarchical nature of Doms and subs with a lot of boot licking. We cast our eyes at the floor if we couldn't gaze at a Top's leather boots. Bottoms didn't talk or even ask questions unless a Top formally recognized them. Although I didn't have any interest in becoming a slave, I did enjoy the Master/slave atmosphere and found the scene erotically arousing. Those who were committed to being in a Master/slave relationship no doubt both felt the sexual excitement and saw it as formal training into the Master/slave lifestyle. The men who played at these occasional parties were among the most serious leathermen in San Francisco; my attendance at these events helped me become one of them.

After I had been coming to the parties for about eighteen months, I was invited to sit at the head table. That was quite an honor and an affirmation that I had become a respected "boy" in the leather community. It was an even greater honor, because most men at the head table were Tops, and a few were recognized as Masters. Knowing the importance of propriety, I didn't want to mess up, so I didn't smoke any marijuana and drank very little. Although I loosened up a little at the next party, I was still careful to follow all the rules of decorum. The third time I was at the head table, however, I messed up. I had smoked too much marijuana and quickly forgot all about formality. Then, to make matters even worse, I washed down a large portion of spaghetti with several glasses of wine. I remember becoming extremely sick, and before I could excuse myself, I vomited on the table, committing a serious act of indiscretion, if not sacrilege. I wasn't invited to a party for several months after that. Even when I started attending them again, I was never again invited to sit at the head table.

Pornographic novelists have often portrayed Masters and their slaves as prominent in the leather scene in the late 1960s and early 1970s. The rules between Masters and slaves, so the story goes today, were quite rigid; Doms had all the power and the subs were required to do whatever they were told. This impression of the "Old Guard" was somewhat evident in the fairly strict protocol in the leather bars and by the assumption that the men in those bars lived much of their daily lives in the same hierarchical way. A few men like Bill Bliss and Jim Kane and their slaves Bill Meyer and Ike Barnes became the models for this idealized picture. In reality, however, these Master/slave relationships, though well known in the leather community, were rare. Heavy-duty sadomasochistic play was present in these Master/slave houses, but was not really central in the leather community as a whole.

Chapter 5: MOTORCYCLE CLUBS AND RUNS

The early leather community manifested itself more visibly in the motorcycle clubs than in the Master/slave families with their dungeons. We bonded together on bike runs. I explored this motorcycle scene with Billy Lytton, whom I met very early at Febe's. Unlike Thom Gunn and Bill Bliss, who were considerably older and well established in the leather community, Billy Lytton was only twenty-five years old. He was a strikingly handsome man with blond hair and blue eyes, dressed in full leather and wearing the colors of the Warlocks, one of the most exclusive of the Bike clubs. Their insignia had wings that formed a "W." I fell in love with him almost immediately.

We began hanging out together, and he introduced me not only to the Warlocks, but also to men in other motorcycle clubs in San Francisco – the Barbary Coasters, the San Franciscans, the CMC (California Motor Club), and some others. There were probably about twenty gay motorcycle clubs in the late 1960s. Since I didn't have a motorcycle, Billy introduced me to the Koalas, a unique motorcycle club in San Francisco, because you couldn't be a member if you actually owned a motorcycle. Members of the Koalas would go to leather events, buddy-riding with someone who was a member of another club. I became instantly popular with the Koalas in part because they knew that Billy, a member of the Warlocks, would be attending their events.

Sex with Billy was exciting because he was adventurous and, with my prodding, willing to explore SM activities, particularly whipping ass. But he also loved light bondage, especially handcuffs and nipple play. He was a very good Top, very considerate — almost too considerate. He didn't have the raw masculinity of Tom Gunn, who totally took charge and would tell me what to do. With Billy, it was more exploration. I often encouraged him to try new BDSM activities. He almost always liked them and gradually, with my encouragement, became more assertive and dominant.

The major events of the motorcycle clubs were their "runs." The club's road captain would choose a route along a scenic California highway to a campground. In addition to the Koala and Warlock runs, I also went with Billy to the Satyrs runs in 1966, 1967, and 1968. The Satyrs were the first gay motorcycle club in the nation, founded in 1954 in Los Angeles. They invited the motorcycle clubs in Northern California to join them at their annual gatherings in the mountains near Fresno. All during the day on Saturday there were competitive biking events including speed races, obstacle courses, motocross, and buddy riding. You got points for coming in first, second, or third in each event, and the guys who got the most points would get trophies. These trophies were much prized and quite enormous. Although Billy and I did win a couple of heats in buddy-riding contests, we never won any of these cherished prizes.

In fact, the only prize I ever won was at a run of the Koalas in the Santa Cruz Mountains in 1967, when I won the booby prize for the least attractive meal set-up. Billy and I had stopped at Safeway and bought a bottle of wine that we drank out of a couple of metal cups, washing down our bologna sandwiches, served on cheap, paper napkins. Most of the other guys spent considerable time preparing for a special picnic. Some even packed their saddlebags with special china and polished silverware. That day Bill Bliss and his slave Bill Myers won the prize for best set-up. In addition to special plates, silverware, and an exquisitely prepared meal, they had even brought a chandelier, which they hung from an overhanging branch of a pine tree.

At the Satyrs' run the same year, I remember participating in a couple of buddy-riding contests, but primarily sitting around drinking beer and wine and cheering the winners of the motorcycling events. Gay sex in those days was illegal, and you could go to prison for sodomy; that even included oral sex. Police could and did raid our leather bars at any time and arrest us. It wasn't until 1975 that the powerful Democratic Assemblyman, Willie Brown, authored and got the State Assembly to pass the Consenting Adult Sex Bill that legalized homosexual acts in California. For this Brown earned the enduring support of the gay community in San Francisco, helping him become the City's forty-first mayor in 1996. In 1967, however, we were sexual outlaws, and these early gay motorcycle runs were especially exciting and liberating, because we could express our sexuality openly outdoors in nature. Being outside the law helped forge a strong brotherhood where we supported one another. Gay sex was probably even more exciting because it was socially forbidden. We were truly outlaws – sexual outlaws on bikes.

At these leather runs I loved being among all the sexy masculine guys who dressed in leather and wore shined boots. In those days I was always looking for a Top to fuck me and to take me to a leather event on his Harley-Davidson or BMW. I particularly enjoyed riding with Billy Lytton, who I thought was the most attractive and hottest guy around. He was my ideal type – tall, blond, and muscular, with piercing blue eyes. Sex with him was terrific. I loved being his "boy" and sucking his cock, often publicly at the runs. With my encouragement, he loved beating my ass, increasing our lust for each other.

Very few guys in the motorcycle clubs in these early days were into BDSM, but there were some. At the old-style bike runs, like those of the Satyrs, the competitive events took place all day Saturday. After dinner there would be a ceremony where the judges would award the prizes and trophies. Interestingly, these old-style bike runs also included drag shows, but they were different from the drag shows in the clubs, where gay men were trying to make themselves up in hyper-feminine clothing and make-up. The drag shows at the leather runs really parodied the traditional drag queen shows, with men wearing wigs and gowns, but also sporting hairy legs and beards. These mock drag shows were fun and provoked a lot of laughter. On reflection I now see how these mock drag shows also emphasized the masculinity of gay leathermen. The gay leather community after World War II underscored masculinity, consciously contrasting with society's image of homosexuals as effeminate men who became hairdressers, florists, and interior decorators.

After the drag show, there was a lot of drinking and sex. I remember Billy and me going off into the woods by ourselves so that he could beat my ass. A few others who wanted leathersex, BSDM, and Master/slave play also went off into the woods. The bike culture at this time didn't really support bondage and sadomasochism, though everything was tolerated, if not publicly displayed. I never saw BDSM sex play done openly at a bike run until the late 1970s. So, in 1966, Billy and I went off from the main group into the woods. Billy would whip my ass, and I would suck his dick and get fucked. We weren't the only ones. There were at least three other couples who also went off into the woods. Even among those of us in the woods, BDSM activity was private, and no one intruded on the others' scenes. Everyone saw us go and obviously heard all the slapping noises coming from the ass beating. So they knew we were in the woods playing. When we came back they often made snarky comments, such as, "Why are you guys sneaking off into the woods by yourselves?" I remember responding to one guy who asked us why we didn't play with everyone else: "When you're man enough, come join us." I always felt that being able to take a beating marked me as masculine, just like Alan Ladd's whipping in *Botany Bay* marked him as a tough masculine hero. For a few of us, BDSM naturally fit into the leather world, a place where one could simultaneously celebrate masculinity and homosexuality.

Each year at the end of September, The California Motor Club put on the biggest and most popular leather event in San Francisco, the CMC Carnival. Anyone could buy a ticket for the day's events. The CMC got a one-day liquor permit to sell tickets for drinks. I attended every one of them from the first in 1967 until the last one in 1986. The CMC rented Seamen's Hall in San Francisco until the crowds became overwhelming. The first floor of the hall was packed with hot male bodies. It was an incredible orgy. Eventually, liability insurance and public sex began to concern the people in charge of renting Seamen's Hall, and they decided they would no longer allow the CMC to use their property. At the last CMC carnival in 1986, the organizers were able to rent an empty garage that had been the yellow cab company's headquarters, and a huge crowd packed the area.

Throughout the 1970s, the CMC organizers held a leather contest to choose Mr. CMC Carnival. This may have been the earliest leather contest in the nation; it was certainly the first in San Francisco, and it predated International Mr. Leather (IML) and any other leather contests that I know about. The CMC gave the winner a special leather vest that he would proudly wear the next year in the leather bars and at bike runs. The contest was based entirely on looks and on how sexy the men were, so most wore nothing but a jockstrap and their leather jackets and boots. The contestants would turn around and show their hot asses and some would flirt with the crowd and even play with their cocks through their jocks. Even though the CMC Carnival ended in 1986, it became a model for such massive BDSM/leather street fairs as the Folsom Street Fair and the Up Your Alley Fair, that began on Ringold St. and later moved to Dore Alley.

The Koalas organized themselves very much like all the other bike clubs. We had a president, a vice president, a road captain, and a master-at-arms. We went to the runs of other clubs, but also maintained our own identity and even had our own runs, where we invited guys from other clubs to take us on their motorcycles. There were sixteen full members of the club, with a lot of other friends, including a couple of women. Henri Leleu, who was president of the club when I joined, took a now well-known photograph of all sixteen club members wearing our club colors.* Henri was born in America, though both his parents had emigrated from France. He became an important political organizer of the gay community in San Francisco and was politically active until his death in 1996. The San Francisco GLBT archives have his collected papers, super-8 films, and other pictures of the Koalas.

Our other very famous member was Peter Marino, who was our Road Captain. Peter went to the opera and symphony in a full leather black coat with tails, a black leather tie, and high leather boots. His leather coat was trimmed with ermine at the collar and had rabbit fur sleeves. Peter's wealth allowed us to hold an extravagant second anniversary dinner of the Koalas in 1967 at Fugazi Hall in the North Beach District. Centrally placed in the Hall was a fountain with champagne and gin (French 75's). In the center of the fountain was an ice-

---

*The photograph is on the front cover of this book. I'm in the front row on the far right.

sculpture of the much-reproduced *Leather David*. The meal itself was equally extravagant with many exquisitely prepared courses. Slightly later that year, as the Northern California representative for Warner Bothers Records, Peter signed an exclusive contract with the Grateful Dead. That became the occasion for a truly spectacular party in the spring of 1967. There were artists, musicians, Grateful Dead fans, hippies, straight executives, gay queens, men and women, straights and gays. He also invited the Koalas, so we arrived in our leather uniforms, adding to the mix. There was LSD in the punch and marijuana in the brownies. About 1:00 a.m. the Grateful Dead came out for a spontaneous jam session. Without any doubt, this was the most remarkable party I have ever attended. It didn't end until dawn. Needless to say, I was totally wasted. The next day I called my manager at Merrill Lynch, telling him I wouldn't be in. He asked me whether I was sick. I replied, "No, I'm getting well." He said I'd still have my job, and I hung up the phone.

For a couple of years, being a member of the Koalas' Motorcycle Club centered me in the leather community. We formed a tight-knit brotherhood, watched each other's backs, and played hard together. The Koalas, like the other motorcycle clubs, provided strong support for its members and for others in the leather community. For example, in 1968, when Billy Lytton got into his serious motorcycle accident and was hospitalized, the club held benefits to support his medical care. Unfortunately, Billy's accident ended our close sexual relationship, just as it was becoming more serious. The accident left him permanently disabled, and he left California to go home and be cared for by his family. The club provided important support while he was still immobilized in the hospital, and he used some of the funds we raised to get back to his family.

When I had first joined, the dress code of the Koalas was fairly lax. We could dress casually in Levis, and we wore our "colors," our club insignia, on a cut-off Levi vest over our leather jackets. Later, the club adopted a more formal uniform — wheat-colored Levis with wheat-colored jackets to match. Many of my friends in the club hated the new dress code, but no one wanted to make it a big issue, so we all went along with it, even though it changed the more casual ambiance in the club.

Shortly after Billy's accident, I got into trouble with the Koalas and was forced to resign. After I was in San Francisco for six months, my good friend Andre arrived and began living with me. Although Andre enjoyed the leather scene and at first participated in it, he gradually became more interested in the world of drag. I often went to the drag shows to support him in competitions. In those days, however, the world of the drag queens and that of the leathermen were like oil and water — they didn't mix, kept apart by animosities from both sides. Drag queens were wary of men who practiced Dominance and submission; leathermen wanted to distance themselves from the identification of homosexuality with femininity.

Although the worlds of drag queens and leathermen didn't often intersect, one fall night in 1968 at a drag club I became a lightning rod. I was there in the audience to support Andre in one of his competitions. Earlier that evening I had been at a Koala club meeting and was therefore still wearing the wheat-colored Levis and jacket that sported the club's colors. Near the end of the evening, Andre, who Master of Ceremonies, announced all the awards, including one for the best leather "run show." All the leather clubs were automatically entered in this contest. I was the only Koala present when Andre announced that the Koalas had won the award and so I walked up on stage and accepted it.

When I walked into the club meeting a few days later I was totally shunned. No one talked to me or even looked at me. I was blindsided and had not suspected that I had done anything wrong. Many of the club's leaders thought I had betrayed them by wearing the club's colors on stage at a drag show. The icy stares from nearly everyone utterly unnerved me. One would think that I had murdered one of my brother leathermen. When I understood the supposedly horrid transgression I had committed in their eyes, I was initially visibly shaken. Within a couple of minutes, however, I felt my Irish anger begin to rise. I had been a member of this club for over two years, and now these supposed brothers were shunning me for accepting an award at a drag show. I have never liked conformity or senseless rules. Above all else, I am a man who has always hated artificial boundaries that kept groups of people apart. I had become best friends with a black man when I was on an Air Force base in racist Biloxi, Mississippi, and I was not going to abandon him now for following his own authenticity by becoming a drag queen.

So I took off the jacket with the club insignia and I walked off. I still remained friends with many of the Koalas. The members were divided on my ouster, and many disliked the formality and rigid dress code in the club. Within a year of my leaving the club the Koalas disbanded.

I continued going to leather bars and frequently rode home on motorbikes with leather Tops such as Thom Gunn. And I still went to Bill Bliss's leather parties, playing hard as a bottom pig in his dungeon. Leather and BDSM remained important in my life, but I also began exploring other exciting parts of the San Francisco scene in the late 1960s and early 1970s.

Chapter 6: DRAG QUEENS, HIPPIES, AND DRUGS

Although Andre and I were not lovers, we had a deep friendship and were again housemates. When I had walked through the streets of Biloxi, Mississippi, with him I discovered the virulence of racism in our society, and my perception of American culture changed. In New York City, he had helped me recover from my scars of sexual abuse. Our friendship went deep. With Andre I learned to put myself in someone else's shoes so that their struggles became my own. Before Andre's arrival I had explored the leather world and now I took him to my favorite bars and shared my world with him. Simultaneously, his interests as a gay man of color began to open up new experiences for me.

Andre was a handsome black man, who looked quite stunning wearing leather — jacket, boots, and vest. When he walked into the Tool Box, heads turned. He was one of the few men who comfortably switched roles at that time. When he wore his keys on the left in a leather bar, he could take almost any boy home with him; when he wore them on the right, Tops would compete to take him home. I would watch him move around the bar, conversing with men, eventually taking control of some bottom boy, and making him kneel down before him. While the boy waited, Andre would nonchalantly talk with men around him. When he played the part of a bottom, he would often go home with some hot Top and then end up turning the tables and fucking him.

More than anything Andre loved the theatrics of role-playing; that excited him sexually more than anything else. So it was no real surprise when he began gravitating more to the drag scene, which was all about drama, cross-dressing to perform the part of a rich woman in charge of her life, and then teasing that role to play at the edge of realism and camp. When the audience watched "her," they saw a gay man questioning gender roles, class, sexuality, and social mores.

Although my sexual interests remained centered in the leather world, I enjoyed going with Andre to the Gilded Cage, because I liked watching him perform. I loved the way he played with the audience and had them laughing one moment and enchanted the next. I found it interesting and a lot of fun. I also began to think more about gender and what it meant to be gay.

One Friday night when Andre and I were exploring nightlife at the Gilded Cage, two young, cute guys on weekend leave from Travis Air Force Base came into the bar. Since they were closeted in the military, they were a bit on-edge, but clearly excited as well. I thought back to the time when Andre and I had entered a gay bar in Biloxi. Even though they were not wearing uniforms, their military haircuts gave them away. Andre and I instinctively knew they were in the military and began a conversation with them. They relaxed when they realized that they were safe and no longer had to pretend to be straight. Like a lot of gay men who find themselves at home in the gay community after a lifetime of pretending, they now let their feminine mannerisms emerge. They didn't have anywhere to stay that night, so we invited them to crash at our place. Roberto Landin's family had immigrated to Nantucket from the Azores, islands that are part of Portugal, while Bobby Mendez's family had come from Mexico. Just as the military had thrown Andre and me together as "brothers," we called

Bob and Bobby "the *mijos*," even though only one of them grew up speaking Spanish; the other spoke Portugese and English at home. Whenever they came to San Francisco on furlough, they stayed with us. Six months later, when they were both kicked out of the military for being gay, they moved in with us and we became a "family." Being intimate with three men of color expanded my experiences in the gay community even more.

Although I tried to cross-dress a couple of times, I instinctively knew it wasn't a part of me. I didn't look the part and felt quite silly. Roberto couldn't do drag much better than I could. Although he had female mannerisms, his hairy, masculine build just didn't work, since drag was judged by realism at the time. He probably could have fit in today with the Sisters of Perpetual Indulgence, but not in the drag style of the late 1960s. Bobby was a fairly good drag performer, but Andre was exceptional, looking somewhat like a young Dionne Warwick or Aretha Franklin. He not only looked the part of a sexy woman when he was up on stage, but he had a style to go with it. "Camp" came naturally to him; he both performed and exaggerated gender, class, and race. He had a marvelous voice and could really do female impersonation when singing. When the audience watched him perform, they saw a successful, black diva, but they also laughed as they realized that appearance and reality are not quite the same. In those days, at least, gay men of color seemed particularly drawn to drag. For a moment a black man could become a rich woman in charge of her life, even while recognizing and critiquing the reality of a class-based, heterosexist culture, where appearance and reality were two different things. The world of drag was a parody and exaggeration of heterosexual norms of femininity and masculinity. As such, it provided a gay critique of straight cultural values by poking fun at them. At the same time, however, gay men could achieve cultural success through artistic symbolism and performance.

The world of the drag queens really exploded a few times a year when "balls" were held at the Gilded Cage and other venues. The Halloween Ball was by far the largest and became one of the major events in gay San Francisco of the late 60s and 70s. The King and Queen of the Imperial Court would oversee the festivities, most of which consisted of contests that involved various performances. Prizes were offered for stylized dancing, called voguing, for singing, for costumes, and for many other categories. The weeks before the Halloween Ball were therefore very busy at our house, as we all pitched in helping Andre and Bobby assemble their costumes. We all discussed the competitions, and Andre was particularly excited, practicing his singing and dancing.

Although I didn't cross-dress or act feminine, I discovered that a lot of the "straight" men who were in the sweater bars and even the drag bars actually preferred a cute boy type to a man wearing a wig and a dress, so I always got my share of tricks. I began enjoying this scene — I was, after all, on the hunt for hot, butch men. Frankly, I wanted to suck the cocks of masculine men, have them play with my dick, and occasionally get fucked.

Most of the leathermen I knew at that time could not understand my attraction to the world of drag. I wasn't the only leatherman who occasionally hung out at drag shows or went to the more vanilla gay bars. When we saw each other at the Gilded Cage or the Rendezvous, however, we ignored each other. They did not want to be recognized as a leatherman in a sweater bar any more than I did. For the most part I was able to keep the two gay worlds compartmentalized, until that moment when I accepted the trophy at a drag show and was forced to resign from the Koalas. I both understand and identify with those who want to live their lives as masculine gay men, and I don't like to be stereotyped as a fairy. But Andre's life and aspirations taught me an even deeper lesson about stereotyping. In being authentic to ourselves, we must also give space to others to be true to themselves.

Andre and the *mijos* taught me to appreciate and respect that all of us in the gay world have had different family, racial, and cultural experiences. The more they became a part of my life, the more I needed to support them in being authentic to themselves and their dreams, even while I remained true to myself. I understood how hard it was to be a person of color in white America, and that included the gay world as well. I began to appreciate, if I didn't totally understand, that some men and women needed to express a gender identity other than the one assigned at birth. I learned to accept a feminine side of myself as I watched Andre and Bobby perform gender, race, and sexuality in drag. When the Koalas expected me to confess my shame at being present at a drag show wearing the club colors, I didn't hesitate to choose diversity and my gay family over what I perceived to be rigid conformity.

Later in my life, when a controversy arose within the leather community about whether or not a transgender male should be accepted as a gay leatherman, I fought for inclusion. When a few leather clubs decided to exclude transgender men who were not male at birth, I resigned my membership from those groups. Today, all the major leather organizations accept trans men into their clubs and events. I am proud if my leadership and support helped that happen more quickly. I can thank Andre and the *mijos* for giving me an early opportunity to begin to understand that some folks need to transition away from their assigned gender in order to be authentic. I eventually concluded, however, that the feminized gay world was not really my home. The campy way of speaking, calling each other "girls" and "honey," began to grate on me. As much as I had bonded with Andre and the *mijos*, I realized that the drag world was really not my world.

I had left New York because I wanted to join a thriving gay men's leather community, and I was not disappointed. In the year after my arrival I watched the leather scene explode from a couple of leather bars and a few bike clubs to become a mecca for masculine gay men with more than a dozen bars on the Miracle Mile of Folsom Street. Membership in the gay bike clubs exploded and the CMC grew spectacularly. The more intimate leather runs continued, but the CMC Carnival became a public celebration of the leather world.

Cultural change in San Francisco was, however, much broader than leathermen and drag queens. In 1967, the year after I arrived in San Francisco, the hippie movement exploded into the "Summer of Love." Just as the *Life* magazine article became a catalyst for drawing gay leathermen to San Francisco, other newspaper reports proclaimed that San Francisco was the center of psychedelic drugs, where young men and women could experience an alternate reality and "find themselves." Gurus from India and beat poets challenged the norms of a materialistic society. Counter-culture visionaries told young people to opt out of materialism and to tune in to a deeper reality through mind-expanding drugs. Political activists challenged the social order, and protests of the U.S. war in Vietnam swelled the streets with marches. Political liberation and sexual liberation seemed intertwined, and fucking was even promoted as a political act that would liberate society from oppression. Aided by marijuana and LSD, a psychedelic art scene flourished.

While I had come to San Francisco to become part of the leather culture, I found the hippie scene enticing, parts of it quite attractive. On sunny weekend days, I often went to Golden Gate Park. The cultural styles of the leather world and the hippie world were totally different. Hippies all had long hair and wore bright colorful clothing; leathermen wore their hair short and were dressed in black leather. Marijuana, acid, and other mind-altering substances circulated freely in parks and at concerts. I never saw anyone openly taking drugs or even smoking a joint in a leather bar until the late 1970s, when it became more common. Although the majority of the hippies were heterosexual and often quite prejudiced against gay men and lesbians, they usually felt fine allowing everyone to "do their own thing."

By the spring of 1967 Andre and I began to go to be-ins and musical events in Golden Gate Park. Almost everyone there wore bright-colored clothing and had long hair. My close-cropped hair was out of place among hippies, who were listening to music, smoking marijuana, and taking LSD. Working for stockbrokers at Merrill Lynch required me to wear short hair, as did the ethos of the leathermen's culture. So I bought an expensive wig from Woolworth's and transformed myself from a stockbroker and leatherman to a hippie when I wanted to hang out at musical venues in Golden Gate Park.

We were young and rebellious. From our perspective, mainstream culture was oppressive. Even though I was working at Merrill Lynch, I never bought into the materialism of a capitalist society. As a gay man I had experienced the rigidity of social norms that condemned me. I had experienced the attempts of people to change my behavior by shaming me for acts that did not seem shameful to me. I had seen virulent racism directed at me personally for having a black friend when I was in Biloxi. So I was attracted to the hippie message of freedom, a freedom to live life without paying any attention to those who wanted to put us in straightjackets, a freedom to throw off the shackles of conformity and commercialism, a freedom to live a life of love for ourselves and others. I had come to San Francisco "to do my own thing" and now found a movement that encouraged me to be free by rebelling against social pressures and cultural norms.

After the *mijos* began living with Andre and me, the four of us often ended up in Golden Gate Park on nice days attending the "be-ins." The battle cry of "sex, drugs, and rock and roll" resonated with me on many levels. Sexual freedom would allow me and other gay men and lesbians to make love as we wished. Timothy Leary and other apostles of spiritual liberation promised that drugs would open up new vistas where we would feel a unity with nature, a love for others, and even an ecstatic union with the Divine. The music of the Beatles, Rolling Stones, Grateful Dead, and many lesser-known bands allowed us to dance with Dionysian abandon, forging a community where birth and status no longer mattered.

Looking back over my years of taking drugs, I need to differentiate the early days when I was primarily smoking marijuana and taking LSD from the later times when we were using every kind of drug imaginable, including mood enhancing drugs like cocaine, speed, and tranquilizers. In the early days the psychedelic experiences were exhilarating and quite positive. "Mind-blowing" has become a cliché, but my first experiences with LSD truly shattered my everyday reality in quite uplifting ways. I sucked on the blotter that had a dot of acid on it and my perception of the world changed. When I was at be-ins in Golden Gate Park, I remember seeing the trees and rhododendron bushes become part of me. The whole universe opened up; I soared with the pigeons into the clouds. I shared communion with the other hippies as we danced. As I whirled in an ecstatic dance, I felt a deep sense of love for all beings and all life. Colors vibrated, and I perceived them as tastes and smells. Although these spiritual experiences have dimmed over time, they are still part of me. Unfortunately, the spiritual exhilaration of the Summer of Love rapidly faded. We wore out our bodies with cocaine and speed, desperately seeking a state of permanent ecstasy. Feeling good became a goal in itself, and the early gurus of LSD, mescaline, and marijuana no longer mentored us to spiritual heights.

Although the hippies proclaimed sexual liberation, they weren't particularly enlightened about homosexuality. For the most part, straight males were threatened by the presence of gay men, who were sexually interested in hooking up with other men. So we naturally gravitated toward other gay men at those hippie gatherings. Our sexual freedom meant dancing and listening to rock music with other gay men. We took mind-expanding drugs and hung out together. And, of course, we had sex together.

Andre, the *mijos*, and I found a small after-hours club where gay hippies would go late at night. The place was called Doyel's after the name of the owner of the small storefront of about 1500 square feet. Inside the building, located at 1665 Market Street near Gough, were a small bar and a large open space that served as a dance floor when it wasn't too crowded. The place probably held about seventy-five people. Psychedelic and political posters covered the front glass windows, allowing for privacy. The other popular after-hours club was The Big Basket. Gay and straight hippies partied at both places from 1:00 to 6:00 a.m., mingling, dancing, and celebrating — "grooving" as we said in late 1960s and early 70s. Gay bartenders often went to Doyel's when they closed their bars at 2:00 a.m. Alcohol was served in styrofoam cups. LSD, mescaline, and other psychedelic drugs were available and commonly used. Uppers and downers were freely shared among the patrons.

Gay men in leather mingled with drag queens. Rock stars, actors, and professional dancers all showed up. I remember seeing the ballet virtuoso Rudy Nureyev partying at Doyel's in July 1967. That same weekend Andre and I attended a private party that was raided by the police. While we escaped by going onto the roof and down a fire escape, Nureyev, along with his dance partner Margot Fonteyn, were arrested as the *San Francisco Chronicle* reported. Anyone of any sexual orientation who was looking for a late-night party found it at Doyel's, and if you were a gay hippie, this was your place.

The drug scene at Doyel's got more extreme toward the end of the 1960s. Doyel locked the door to his bedroom upstairs, so no one could enter without his permission, but gay hippies passed out in the bathroom and on the stairway. The last time I partied at Doyel's, he had put out a huge bowl of "Christmas Trees" (a combination of speed and a barbiturate) that kept the patrons awake, yet relaxed, all night long. "Christmas Trees" were the street name of clear capsules of Dexamyl, with green and white beads inside. That night you could just reach in the bowl and take what you wanted instead of paying the usual price of two for a dollar.

Sometime in the summer of 1968 I met Don Folkers, who eventually became one of the great loves of my life. I walked into Club Rendezvous, a gay bar on Sutter Street, which we leathermen derisively called a "sweater bar." Don was one of the bartenders there. For me it was love at first sight. He knew I was interested in him, as I hung out at the bar the whole night and many subsequent nights. He clearly enjoyed my attention and played me like a harp, flirting just enough to keep me interested, but then backing off and becoming inaccessible. I knew that I wouldn't be going home with him, because he was dating Doyel, the tall, charismatic gay hippie who owned and ran the after-hours club on Market Street. When we chatted, we were always on the same wavelength. We continued the camaraderie, often enjoying each other's company at Doyel's in the fall of 1968.

By late November 1968, however, everything began falling apart. The drug scene was out of control, and drugged hippies near death were taken to San Francisco General Hospital. One of the last times I partied at Doyel's was the night of the Humphrey vs. Nixon presidential election. I was high on both acid and "Christmas Trees." I was so stoned that I barely made it back to my place at about 5:00 a.m. In the back of my dazed mind I knew that I had to get to work — I couldn't get away with skipping work again, even though I was totally wasted. Somehow I was able to drag myself to work. The previous night all of us at Doyel's had thought that Humphrey had won the election, and I wasn't about to hear otherwise, totally ignoring the latest returns. So at work, in spite of the evidence, I pugnaciously argued with the mostly Republican stockbrokers that Humphrey had won.

How I made it through the day and got back to our flat I'll never know. Exhausted, I collapsed on the bed, waking up the next morning feeling dreadful. Again I went to work. By the end of the week I admitted to myself that I needed to change my life. I was wasted on drugs and was having a "freak-out," the hippie term at the time for psychotic episodes caused by taking drugs. I knew I had to get away from San Francisco and the drug scene, so I arranged a transfer to the Merrill Lynch office in New York, so that I could dry out. At about the same time Don had his own "freak out" and landed in San Francisco General Hospital. Both Don's and my drug-related nervous breakdowns occurred a month before Doyel himself freaked out. After going to my mother's place down the Peninsula, where she took care of me for three days, I headed out to New York City by myself, rented a small apartment, and again began working as an analyst at Merrill Lynch.

After working the month of December in New York City, I was able to take a two-week vacation and went back to San Francisco to get my affairs in order so Andre and the *mijos* could find a new roommate for the apartment. While cleaning out my stuff with Andre, I talked about my need to get away from San Francisco. Andre began thinking that he might want to go back to New York City with me. The *mijos* also thought that it might be a good idea if they came along as well.

One evening, only a few days after I was back in San Francisco, we got a call that Doyel was in bad shape and freaking out. Andre and I went over to see if we could help. Everyone else had left the party by the time we arrived, and everything was a mess. Doyel was at the top of the stairs yelling incoherently. I pleaded with him to come downstairs, telling him that we would take care of him. He quieted down and seemed to listen for a moment, but when he spoke again his reply was unintelligible. Suddenly he became maniacal and started throwing things over the balcony onto the dance floor. We dodged the full aquarium as it crashed onto the floor, spilling rocks, water, and flying fish in all directions.

"We're your friends," Andre pleaded. "You need to get help. We can take you to the emergency room." That only enraged him more. Doyel continued babbling, sometimes saying he didn't know us, and then muttering that the bar was now closed. I realized that our presence was not helping him and was probably only making things worse. I tried one more time to calm him, but he only got angrier. He began throwing books over the edge and toppled a bookshelf over. "It's your place and you can do what you want, but I don't have to be here," I yelled up at him. Getting no response, we left to get help.

Doyel escalated things almost immediately after we left. He lit something, perhaps accidentally, and the curtains started burning, then the building was blazing. Doyel stripped off all his clothes, jumped on his motorcycle, and rode down the street stark naked, finally crashing the bike. Although badly bruised, he didn't have any serious injuries. The cops took him to jail and charged him with arson, and he eventually ended up in a psych ward in the hospital at Sedro Woolly, Washington, near his childhood home. The macabre image of Doyel's bar in flames with its naked owner roaring down the road on a motorcycle is emblematic of the gruesome end of a naïve era of hippie idealism.

Andre and the *mijos* decided to go back with me to New York. We would leave the heavy San Francisco drug scene behind and try to get our lives back in order. Now in earnest, we all began clearing out the apartment, storing some things and junking much more. In those days you could get cars from dealers and rental agencies to drive back to the East Coast. We got a car, loaded it with some essentials, and headed out to New York. Andre had called his mother in Newark, New Jersey. "Of course you can come live with me," she immediately offered. "You're family! There's plenty of room in the basement. Come and stay as long as you want."

Barry & Peter at the Empire State Building, 86th floor
July 1958, *Private Collection of Peter Fiske*

Peter's 10th Grade High School Photo
June 1960, *Private Collection of Peter Fiske*

Peter in the United States Air Force
June 1962, *Private Collection of Peter Fiske*

Peter at Rockaway Beach, New York
June 1969, *Private Collection of Peter Fiske*

Colt Thomas, Charlie Smith, and Al Parker
at the SF Leather Daddy's Boy Contest held at the SF Eagle
September 1983, *the Robert Pruzan Collection,*
Courtesy of Gay, Lesbian, Bisexual, Transgender Historical Society

Peter at home, San Francisco
March 1984, *Private Collection of Peter Fiske*

Peter in California Highway Patrol Uniform, San Francisco
June 1986, *Private Collection of Peter Fiske*

Peter at the Folsom Street Fair, San Francisco
September 1987, *Private Collection of Peter Fiske*

Peter at Stonewall 20th Anniversary San Francisco LGBT Pride
June 1989, *Private Collection of Peter Fiske*

"Strap," Peter, and Les at Folsom Street Fair, San Francisco
September 1989, *Private Collection of Peter Fiske*

Shadow Morton, Coulter, Sky Renfro, Peter, and John
at Folsom Street Fair, San Francisco
September 1990, *Private Collection of Peter Fiske*

Coulter and Peter at International Mr. Leather (IML), Chicago
May 1991, *Private Collection of Peter Fiske*

Coulter and Peter at International Mr. Leather (IML), Chicago May 1991, *Private Collection of Peter Fiske*

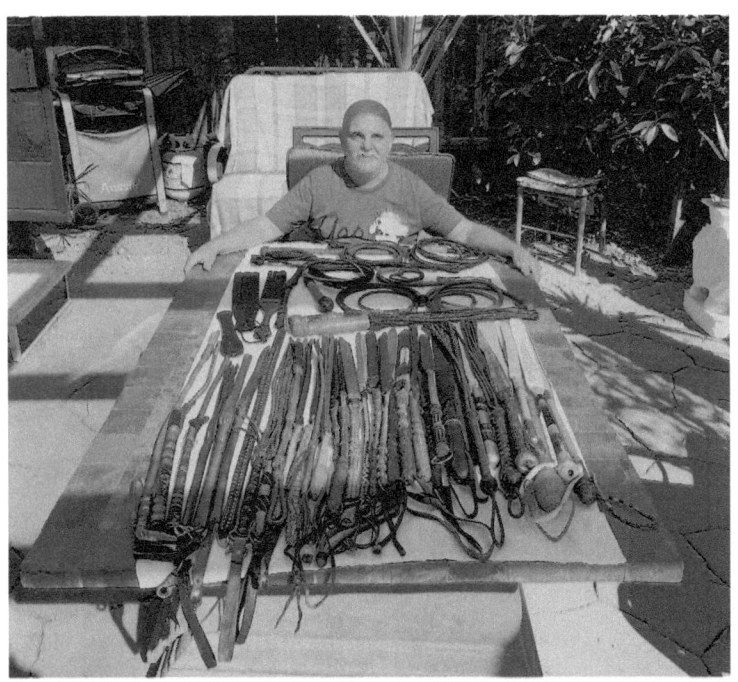

Peter at home with a part of his whip collection, Palm Springs March 2018, *photo by Jacob Hale, Private Collection of Peter Fiske*

Chapter 7: STONEWALL AND SPIRITUAL GROWTH

Andre, the *mijos*, and I arrived in Newark, New Jersey, in the middle of January 1969 after an uneventful quick trip across the country. We took turns sleeping and driving. Andre's mother wouldn't accept any money for rent. "It wouldn't be right to charge rent to family," she said. Of course, we were all generous in giving her money "for groceries," which she gladly accepted. The place in Newark was conveniently located near the PATH (Port Authority Trans Hudson) rapid rail station, so I could quickly and easily get to work at Merrill Lynch. We also took the train to the Christopher Street station when we explored gay New York City on weekends and holidays.

The first weekend after we got settled, I introduced Andre and the *mijos* to a routine I had begun in December. I would first go to one of two leather bars (Danny's or The Stud) in the Christopher Street area, then I would go to the empty meat trucks along the Hudson River on 10th Street, and finally I would end up at the Stonewall Inn. Early in the evening, the first weekend the four of us were back in New York City, we went to Danny's for a couple of hours and had some beers. I had been happily surprised to find leather bars now in New York City. The protocols were the same as those in San Francisco, particularly later in the night when leather guys started cruising more seriously. Early in the evening, however, the atmosphere was more casual. The *mijos*, who were not particularly into the leather world, felt comfortable there, drinking a few beers to begin our night of partying. In the earlier hours there was an unhurried masculine energy that slowly built in hopes of finding the perfect trick later in the evening.

Shortly before midnight, as the electrical energy in the bar was starting to build, the four of us headed out to find a different kind of sex, a pure male sex without any need to flirt or find a perfect partner for the night. We headed over to Tenth Avenue, next to the Hudson River, where empty meat trucks were parked for the weekend. The drivers had rinsed them out and left them open to air out. Now anonymous gay men approached the primal caves of these huge semi-trucks. We could smell the scent of male musk, even from a distance. Or did we just imagine it in our excitement as we approached the trucks? Someone offered a hand and pulled us up into the huge cavern, probably about thirty feet long.

Moving into the shadows, our eyes adjusted. Men leaned against the walls of the truck. Other dark figures were kneeling, taking communion from cocks. The excitement of pure raw sex drew us into the recesses of the truck. I knelt before one phallus and then another. I lost track of time and my body trembled. My dick was hard. I moved from one dark figure to another. Their cocks seemed to shine. At some point in the eternity of moving shadows, I would reach an orgasm, as would most of the guys. The energy would build over and over, my whole body thrilled and vibrated, and sometimes I climaxed again.

The number of men inside one of these trucks varied between twenty and forty. Sometimes the trucks became so crowded that there was hardly space for anything but groping and feeling partially naked bodies. I liked it best when there were fewer men. Sometimes I even wore a leather vest and chaps into the trucks and found other leathermen lurking in the dark recesses. On a couple of occasions, a leatherman took off his belt and whipped my ass as I was sucking on his manhood. These orgies in the meat trucks of New York City took place every weekend. I understand that they lasted all during the 1970s, long after we had left New York City.

A couple of hours later, the four of us were sexually drained. We went back to Christopher Street and I introduced them to what had become my favorite bar in New York City, the Stonewall. We walked up to the door. A doorman opened a window and looked us over. He probably recognized me from previous visits, because he ushered us into the bar without any questioning. There was a three-dollar cover charge, and we each received two coupons for drinks. The street floor had a bar and tables for hanging out; upstairs was a dance floor.

The Stonewall had become my bar in New York, because it was the most diverse gay bar I have ever been in, yet there was a real sense of community. Gay men in drag mingled with guys in street clothes and leather. We all danced and celebrated together late into the night. I loved the bar, because we felt a gay pride and unity there. Andre, the *mijos*, and I got to know many of the people there. I knew two of the drag queens who eventually became famous for instigating the Stonewall riots — Sylvia Rivera and Marsha Johnson, a black transvestite. We were all family, a gay family with every color of the rainbow flag.

In the months before I left New York I was present when police raided the Stonewall three times, and I had learned the drill. When the bartender turned on the bright lights, we all stopped dancing and sat down at the tables. The officers came in and told us to line up and show our IDs. Almost everyone in those days was somewhat closeted — even though I was totally open with friends and family, I could not be openly gay at work and keep my job at Merrill Lynch. If we were arrested, the police would automatically submit our names to the *New York Daily News*. If our employers read that we were arrested "for lewd and lascivious behavior," they would almost always fire us. Guys who were totally closeted with a wife and children had even more at stake.

If the police didn't think that our attire matched the gender on our IDs, they could arrest us. It was the law that you had to have three items of clothing that matched your gender. Drag queens had to strip until the cops could see their jockstraps, male undershirt, and male socks. It was totally demeaning and ridiculous. I felt outraged and violated. We murmured that we should resist this bullshit. There was a lot of anger in the room the last time I was there at a raid just before we left New York City to go back to San Francisco. That time, the police backed off.

I was therefore not surprised that a spark from police harassment at the Stonewall eventually lit the powder keg. As much as we liked New York City, we all felt that San Francisco was really our city. We left New York on June 24, 1969, three days before the Stonewall riots. I heard the news when we were in Joplin, Missouri. I bought a copy of the *New York Times* that had the Stonewall riots as a major front-page story. "Gays Revolting," screamed the headline; "Riots at the Stonewall" stated a smaller caption. I remember my feelings. I was extremely proud that my brothers and sisters had stood up to the authorities. In my mind I was becoming a political activist and would go back to San Francisco, ready to fight for gay rights.

If I had been in New York City, I would have been at the Stonewall and present for that momentous event that changed LGBT history. Although I missed the actual riots, I recently found out that anyone who was present at the Stonewall during a police raid was officially a "Stonewall Veteran." Since I had been present for three police raids, I'm now proud to call myself a "Stonewall Veteran," though I still regret missing the actual event by a few days. At the Stonewall I had felt part of a small, but wonderfully diverse, community of gay men.

When I left New York, I quit the brokerage business altogether. I no longer wanted to work in such a conservative environment, so I didn't try to arrange a transfer. I quickly found a job in the accounting department at UC San Francisco. Soon after arriving back in San Francisco I ran into Don Folkers again. That fall we became very good friends and hung out together in Golden Gate Park and gay bars. He told me his affair with Doyel was finished, and I spontaneously told him that I loved him. He seemed both flattered and amused. Late one night he did come back with me to my place and we fooled around and had sex together, sucking each other off, but no bells or fireworks went off. The next day Don sat me down and gave me a choice. He said we could have a brief sexual affair that would end with us not seeing one another again or we could be best friends for life. But we could not have both. I didn't hesitate for even an instant. I loved being with Don and couldn't imagine my life without him and I immediately said, "I want to be your best friend for life."

That December I got a fairly large bonus from previous work at Merrill Lynch, and Don and I decided to follow other hippies we knew to go live in Hawaii. I took a leave of absence, and with that money Don and I left San Francisco in January 1970 and went to Maui, where we lived with over 500 other hippies in Makena State Park. Most of the hippies there were straight, but we lived with about fifty other gay men on a section of the park called Black Sands Beach.

It was quite an experience. Don and I lived in a one-room, abandoned shack made out of bamboo and rice sacks. We ate fish that we caught, gifts that people brought to us, grocery food that was too old to be sold, and even food from the dump. We also took lots of LSD and other drugs. Many celebrities also spent time there. Jimi Hendrix, the great electric guitar player and rock musician, gave concerts on the beach and passed out LSD. Peter Fonda, brother of Jane Fonda and an actor in Easy Rider, camped there for a while and gave drugs to all of us on the beach. Every night was party time with lots of drugs, sex, and rock and roll.

Although it was an exciting and wild six months, the living conditions were terribly unsanitary, with so many people living together without any bathrooms. Everyone was peeing and shitting in the woods behind the beach in a swampy area with lots of flies and bugs. It's not surprising that we got a very serious case of dysentery after six months. It's really amazing that that we hadn't had any epidemics before that. The dysentery passed from one person to the next until almost everyone was very sick. So, as the health hazards spread, our idyllic, hippie experiment on the beach ended.

Don and I arrived back in San Francisco and took a small apartment on Capp Street in the Mission District with Joe, a friend I had met in New York City a few years earlier. Even though the place was small, we each had a bedroom, and remarkably the place cost only seventy-five dollars a month. We got involved in some of the protests against the Vietnam War and allowed anti-war activists who were fleeing from military service to stay with us. Don brought many one-night stands back to the house. Joe and I occasionally brought someone back as well. So the house was always filled with people, some very interesting. I enrolled at City College, where I studied Latin American studies, history, and art. The Veterans Administration gave me a stipend under the GI Bill so I didn't have to work. After earning sixty credits over a two-year period, I got my AA degree.

We had arrived back in San Francisco just before the first gay pride parade, celebrating the one-year anniversary of the Stonewall Rebellion. It was very personal to me, since the Stonewall was my bar when I was in New York. The march wasn't called "gay pride" that first year, but "gay freedom day." Only four or five hundred gay men and women marched down Polk Street to Aquatic Park, where there was a celebratory picnic. Compared to the huge anti-war marches that we had attended with over 100,000 people, those numbers were small. However, considering that gay men and lesbians were mostly in the closet then, a few hundred gay men and lesbians openly marching down Polk Street in San Francisco made quite a statement. Amazingly, just two years later there were about 100,000 marchers at the Pride Parade and in 1978 there were 500,000 marchers after Anita Bryant started her "Save Our Children" campaign to outlaw employing homosexuals in the classroom. Anita Bryant inadvertently energized the Gay Liberation Front, founded in New York after the Stonewall riots, and it became a powerful force for gay rights. In the same year Harvey Milk campaigned across California to help defeat Proposition 6 (the Briggs Initiative), which would have fired openly gay schoolteachers. Thus, by 1978, the gay pride parade rivaled the anti-war movement protests and made LGBT rights visible and even respectable. We had become a mass movement, and "coming out" events began to change the fight for gay rights forever.

That day in June, 1970, at the first San Francisco Pride March, I vowed to make the fight for LGBT rights central in my life. Except for work, I had been openly gay since moving to San Francisco. Marching as a gay man pushed me even further out of the closet. Along with the other marchers, we were affirming that we would no longer be silent or put up with discrimination, but would openly fight for our human rights when police raided our bars and parties. The Stonewall riots had been the spark that ignited the seething sense of injustice that so many of us had felt in so many ways — in employment, in sexual and social relationships, and in equal justice under the law. I felt that I was not only trying to lead an authentic life, true to myself, but that all of us gay men and lesbians were fighting for the rights of everyone, including those still in the closet.

During this first gay pride parade in San Francisco, I hugged old friends and rubbed my body against strangers as I jostled past them. We drank and spilled beer as we threaded our way through the streets. Joints were passed around as we celebrated the birth of a mass political movement. I was part of an orgasmic celebration.

Later that evening we migrated to Golden Gate Park where gay hippies jammed on drums, while we danced to celebrate gay liberation. Don and I renewed friendships with lots of people that day. The queens were ebullient and outrageously colorful; gay liberation activists were determined and strident. Leathermen and a very few courageous political leaders marched together. That day the gay community had become a mass movement. We had become family.

On a warm day a few months later, Don and I were hanging out with some gay hippies in Golden Gate Park. They were about to go to a fall Hindu festival. It sounded interesting, so we tagged along with them and saw people pulling a bullock cart with huge statues of a Hindu god and goddess through the streets of San Francisco. We joined the procession. I didn't know much about Hinduism, but the festival was quite fascinating. The smell of incense, the sounds of music and chanting, and the sights of dancing men and women in saffron robes surrounded us. At one point the cart hauling the gods started tilting, and people rushed up to steady it. It was quite exotic. I believe the festival had been organized by the Hare Krishnas, who were wearing the long saffron robes. We joined a group of gay men who told us about a guru who ministered to gay hippies. They invited us to his house that evening for dinner and a musical celebration.

We went to the small ashram, which also doubled as the Zen Center in San Francisco, and I was introduced to the man who would become my guru. Sadguru Sant Keshavadas looked intently at Don, Joe, and me, and smiled. For an instant I felt like I was the only person in the room with the guru looking only at me, accepting me without condition. In a bit of a daze I started talking with some of the other people there. One gay guy told me the meaning of the guru's name. "Keshava," he said, could be translated as "long hair" and "das" was servant. The guru's name, according to him, therefore meant "servant to the longhairs" or "guru of the hippies."

People started moving to a table with food, and we filled our plates with yellow rice, lentil stew, a piece of naan, and some pickled vegetables. We sat on the floor, and a gay couple next to us asked us how long we had served the guru. When they learned it was our first time, they began telling us stories about his kindness and emphasized that he was unique in being non-judgmental about homosexuality and open to people of all sexual orientations. An older hippie said that he had been seeking deep spirituality all his life and had finally found it with Keshavadas.

When we were almost finished eating, the music and chanting began. The guru was playing a harmonium, his wife Sita sitting next to him. Someone else was playing a flute, and three others were playing *tablas*, Indian drums. With the music in the background the guru began chanting several mantras, most beginning with "Om," the sacred sound that began all creation in the Hindu universe. Then the guru started teaching. He emphasized that we were beautiful and should meditate to deepen the love within each of us. We were all unique, but we were all part of something greater than ourselves; we were part of God. It wasn't just the words that I found attractive; it was his accepting, loving, and playful manner of speaking. He said that if difficulties get in the way of finding God, we should ask Ganesh to remove the impediments. I later learned that Ganesh is the elephant-headed god who is very popular in Hinduism as the deity who removes obstacles that keep us from accepting our beautiful selves.

Don, Joe, and I found a profound peacefulness in Keshavada's presence that contrasted with so much else in our frenzied lives. I have been interested in spirituality my whole life. When I was an altar boy in my youth I felt drawn to a spiritual reality beyond myself and even seriously entertained the possibility of becoming a priest until I realized that I would have to lie about my sexuality and deny my true nature. My religious experience as a young Catholic opened up the sense that there is something greater beyond myself. For a while I found a deep connection with the universe through mind-expanding drugs and even today feel that my early LSD trips had opened up a beautiful reality where I was intimately connected with nature, plants, animals, and other human beings. Over time, however, the drug scene degenerated into a hedonism that emphasized feeling good for its own sake. The joy I felt in the presence of Sant Keshavadas was a new beginning along a spiritual path. He validated me as a gay hippie, and I felt a beautiful peacefulness mixed with joy. Here was a man from a different culture with different experiences from my own, and he had expressed a deep love for me. He didn't preach a divisive message, but one of acceptance. Remembering his love for me, I have also tried to accept people with experiences different from my own and have fought against restrictive social rules. At the beginning of this century the whole leather community struggled over accepting trans men in male spaces. I fought tirelessly for these men, and our leather world changed for the better for all of us. Sant Keshavadas became a model for my loving all people who were struggling for acceptance.

Over the next few months Don, Joe, and I became regulars at his religious center. We learned the chants, and Keshavadas began to engage us more personally in conversation. Many Indian musicians, including Ravi Shankar, the famous sitar player, held concerts at the ashram. After a couple of months we became regulars at the house, and the guru gave us our personal mantras, the first stage of initiation, where a disciple and guru begin a serious relationship. I occasionally still say mine to this day.

Soon after that Keshavadas suggested that we move into the ashram and become even more involved with his movement. We said we would think it over. In talking about it we realized that moving into the ashram would involve a very serious commitment and eventually entail our going to the guru's main ashram in Bangalore in South India. As much as we were drawn to the Sadguru, we decided that we did not want to make this commitment. I had avoided religious entanglements all my life, because all of them seemed to constrain more than liberate me. We continued to go to the guru's house for celebrations and chanting for several months. The times I spent with Keshavadas were very important to me.

Slowly, the leather community began to take up more time in my life. Through a deep brotherhood with leathermen I discovered my true spiritual journey in life. I began to realize that the spirituality the Hindu guru had been talking about was also present in my connections in the community of leathermen. When I submitted to a Top in leather play I felt my own ego melt away in the dance of Dominance and submission. As I left my socially constructed ego behind, I found an inner beauty within me. Later, when I began to top other men, I felt a deep gratitude for their submission and a humility that also freed me of my superficial ego. The power exchange in our leather play opened up a whole spiritual reality for me. I feel a deep love for every one of my leather brothers and sisters. And when I play, I enter a sacred space of freedom that I usually call catharsis. To me it seems similar to the spiritual liberation that my guru Keshavadas had talked about. Dominance and submission create a power exchange between people that can be deeply liberating. The tension between the man in absolute control and the man who is freely giving himself as a gift becomes a power exchange between the two people where the ego is left behind. It doesn't always happen, but it can if the two men who are playing have a deep trust and respect for each other. Then the superficial ego disappears, and something truly remarkable happens between them. I had felt this dynamic when I had played with Thom Gunn and other leathermen before, and my time with Keshavadas helped me understand it on a deeper level.

Chapter 8: MATURING AS A LEATHERMAN

It has been over fifty years since I walked into the Empire Theatre in 1964 and had my first adult BDSM experience. Since then, leathersex has been a constant in my life, though there were periods, like my time in Hawaii, when I temporarily suspended leather play. Even while attending the musical celebrations and teaching sessions with Sadguru Keshavadas, however, I occasionally played with some terrific Tops. Coming back from Hawaii marked the slow ending of my hippie days and my becoming a more committed leatherman.

I had been an exclusive bottom in Leather play during the late 60s, looking for hot guys to take control. A few months after returning from Hawaii, I had an experience that introduced me to the joys of topping. One Saturday night I went to the Rendezvous, the gay bar where Don was working as bartender. As a "sweater bar," it was not usually a place for picking up tricks for leathersex.

I was chatting with friends, drinking a beer, when a young Marine came in and sidled up to the bar. Conversations halted and all eyes turned to this stocky, muscular man, about twenty years old. His good looks caused everyone to stare at him; it was also unusual to walk into a gay bar wearing a full military uniform. Although I usually liked older men, a man in uniform always got my attention. I moved over beside him and asked, "How are you doing, Marine?" Luckily I have never been shy and had no trouble striking up a conversation. I mentioned that I had been in the military and asked him where he was stationed. Quickly the ice was broken, and the other men in the bar returned to their conversations. As we were casually chatting, I began fantasizing about this uniformed, muscular kid tying me up, beating me, and taking charge sexually. I asked him what he was into. He said he liked ass beating and maybe more. Now I was hooked. He accepted my invitation back to my apartment.

Before we left the bar, he looked into my eyes, slurring his words, "Sometimes when I do things like this, I don't remember anything that happened. And I often get robbed."

"Aaah," I thought, "He wants sex with a man, but can't admit to himself that he's gay." I decided to play his game, though I wasn't sure that I'd actually rob him.

When we arrived back at my place, I unlocked the door and held it open. I followed him in and locked the door. When I turned back to face him, he had already stripped off his uniform and was folding it neatly on a chair by the door. I was astonished at his lightening speed. I watched him quickly strip off his underwear. Then in one smooth movement he threw himself on his knees, sat back on his haunches, and held his thick Marine belt in front of him saying, "O.K. Beat me and fuck me." He bowed his head, and his dick became rigid. So did mine.

Although I had never topped before, I needed no further encouragement. I wanted to beat him as much as I usually wanted to be beaten, or maybe even more. I took his belt and laid it on the kitchen table. "Don't move — stay where you are," I barked. Returning from the bedroom with some rope, I tied his hands behind him and pulled him to his feet. I put my hand behind his neck and pushed him down over the kitchen table. I massaged his firm bubble butt, and gently pushed his legs apart as he moaned. I picked up his belt, doubled it, and cracked it across both cheeks. I got even more turned on as I watched a red stripe appear. He moaned, encouraging me to beat him more. I imagined myself lying across the table and got the same thrill I had as a bottom. I also felt a new power surging through me, knowing that he was at my mercy and wanted me to use him. His moans encouraged me to strap his ass harder, and I slipped more into the zone where only the boy and I existed. The redder his ass became, the more he whimpered with excitement. My own cock strained against my pants, until I kicked them off and stood naked behind him with the belt in my hand. I took a final hard swing and he gasped.

    I spread his legs more and pressed my cock into his crack, feeling the heat of his butt against my thighs. Although I had never fucked anyone before, I knew I wanted to mount his freshly strapped ass, but the table was too high. I lightly wrapped the belt around his neck, pulled him to his feet, and told him I was going to fuck him. He moaned in response. I guided him into my bedroom and pushed him over the edge of the bed with his legs spread wide apart. I fingered his asshole, wetting it with my spit. I swung the belt a few more times. He squirmed, but pushed his ass up toward me. I grabbed his bound hands, pushed his chest firmly onto the bed, and mounted him. He grunted and sighed as I fucked him harder. Soon he convulsed in an orgasm just as I shot my load into him.

    During the night I woke the boy up and fucked him a couple of more times. While he was showering in the morning, I saw his wallet lying on the table beside the bed. I decided to play his game and took twenty dollars from the wallet, leaving him plenty to get back to the Marine base. When he finished showering, he put on his uniform and asked me what we had done together. I answered, "We hung out and had some drinks and you fell asleep." He shook my hand, said "Thank you Sir," and left. I never saw him again. That night something clicked in my brain, and I began a gradual shift from bottom to Top in my BDSM play.

As wonderful as it is to be a bottom, that evening I discovered the equal joy of taking control as a Top. As a bottom I had found a sense of freedom that comes from surrendering. Now as a Top I could identify with the beautiful men who were finding their spiritual liberation through surrender, while simultaneously enjoying the raw power that comes from taking control. This power was balanced by responsibility for the men who trusted me to use it responsibly. Something more powerful than my own petty ego seemed to possess me when I took charge in a BDSM scene. When men surrendered to me, I felt humbled by their respect and trust. When I put aside my ego and took responsibility for another man's well being in an intense BDSM scene, I also experienced catharsis, even if it wasn't always as dramatic as I had felt as a bottom. The exchange of power between two men is, in my experience, deeply spiritual. The liberation I felt both as a Top and as a bottom is really beyond explanation. It can only be experienced and only happens when two men are in harmony.

After living on Capp Street in the Mission for four years, Don, Joe, and I moved to Washburn Alley in the South of Market (SOMA) district, the center of the San Francisco leather scene in the 1970s. I was delighted to find that BDSM play was becoming more open and visible than it had been in the late 1960s. The No Name bar, just down the block from our flat, became one of my favorites. For the first time, Don began going to leather bars to find bottoms for impact play. He quickly became a very popular leather Top and brought many of his tricks back to our apartment. Joe, our other roommate, remained a good friend, but never developed an interest in leathersex, and our lives began drifting apart.

In January 1975 I was standing outside the No Name when a tall man, impeccably dressed in leather and wearing a Muir cap, walked up to the door. Immediately I felt a magnetic pull that drew me into the bar behind him. I walked up next to him and heard him ordering a beer. As he turned to survey the crowd, our eyes immediately connected and I smiled. At that moment I knew that he wanted me as much as I wanted him. Breaking eye contact I moved away, went over to a group of friends, and waited, virtually certain that we'd be going home together. We did and George Benedict became one of the great loves of my life.

Even though I had begun topping after my experience with the Marine, I still bottomed, so I was perfectly content to let George take charge. When we went back to his place, very close to my own apartment in the SOMA district, he quickly stripped me and bound me with rope. There was no hesitation, no wasted effort. As he wrapped the ropes around me and tied the knots, his hands deftly brushed my nipples, cock, and thighs, arousing every part of my body. I had been much more into impact play than bondage, but with George, the bondage took me into a very submissive state. I strained against the rope, as it seemed to tighten around me. The more I struggled, the more the rope cut into me. Finally, I surrendered into my helplessness and felt a strong desire for George to use me however he wanted. To my delight, he was into corporal punishment and soon began busting my balls and torturing my tits. Eventually he had me suck his cock, and I felt an incredible connection when he exploded in my mouth. From the very beginning I trusted him and joyfully surrendered. He was my fantasy lover.

My infatuation with George quickly grew into a full-blown love affair. Although we were never monogamous, I became his partner for the next six years, and he became one of the great loves of my life. He was intelligent and well educated with an MBA from Harvard Business School. Having gone bald at an early age, he had built a very successful hairpiece business, called Mastertouch. I occasionally helped him balance the books and take care of invoices. As his business grew, Don began working for him as a full-time employee, though they had a falling out after a couple of years.

I became part of George's circle of friends that included some of the most prominent San Francisco leathermen of that era, men like Jack Fritscher, Jim Kane, Ike Barnes, and Guy Baldwin. Hank Diethelm, who was then the owner of the Brig, was a particularly close friend, and the three of us spent considerable time together. Six months after meeting George, Don and I moved to Noe Valley with a new roommate, Tom Lemon. At almost the same time George moved to a new apartment on Noe Street, only 100 feet from ours, and I was soon spending more time at his place than at my own.

Although I mostly bottomed for George at first, I had also begun to develop more experience as a Top with guys I picked up in the No Name and other leather bars. I have always loved impact play, especially whipping scenes. As a bottom I loved being bound to a St. Andrew's Cross and getting flogged. Now I discovered the same joy in whipping other men. I rekindled my childhood fascinations with whips. I remembered touching Bronco Charley's bullwhip as I sat on his lap, watching Alan Ladd get whipped in *Botany Bay*, and shopping for whips at Uncle Sam's Umbrella Shop. I had accumulated a few good whips before I met George, and I now began collecting them in earnest, becoming quite proficient in using them.

I learned the names of the master whip makers in the United States and studied the pros and cons of their floggers. I had always loved bullwhips, but had never seen anyone play with them. Their traditional length of fifteen to twenty feet made them impractical for impact play in a BDSM scene. They could only be used outdoors by someone who was extraordinarily skilled. A bullwhip, whose tail or "fall" is cracking greater than the speed of sound, is a dangerous weapon and can do serious harm. One day I saw someone playing with a very short single tail whip, three to four feet in length, and learned that David Morgan made different types of mini bullwhips in Seattle. I ordered one immediately and spent many hours cracking it and practicing my accuracy.

About a year after George and I first met, I brought some of my prized whips over to his house to show him. My enthusiasm was contagious, and George suggested I try them out on him so he could feel the various types of leather — elk, moose, cow, and deer hide. At first I approached this clinically, but after several minutes George became very submissive, while I felt empowered watching him react to the various blows. After that, George began asking me to whip him, and I loved feeling him surrender to me.

George also liked getting fisted. In men, fisting is an activity where the bottom relaxes his anal muscles so that he can take the hand of another man inside him. Although I never wanted to get fisted, George asked me to fist him only a couple of months after we got together. He taught me to push my fingers together, making the fist into a duck's beak, and then very slowly push into the anal cavity. There was a lot of preparation. The Top had to make sure that his fingernails were carefully manicured so there would be no sharp edges. In the 70s most Tops didn't wear latex gloves but fisted the bottom with their bare hands. The bottom needed to clean himself out particularly well, and the Top greased the hole with a lot of lubrication, Crisco in those days.

In late 1975 a private sex club, especially dedicated to fisting, opened up in the SOMA district, though it soon moved to a Victorian house in the Mission. No outside signs identified the place as a sex club. A couple of men guarded the basement door, only admitting those who were known to them. Hank Diethelm had initially invited George, and soon I started going as well. By the time we went to the Catacombs, I had already gotten some experience fisting George.

Unlike some BDSM dungeon play, fisting is a very quiet, introspective activity. Everything about the atmosphere in the Catacombs was quiet and subdued, even the music helped to create an almost religious atmosphere. Men wearing leather harnesses and chaps lay quietly in slings. Tops were taking their time, and everything seemed in slow motion. I especially remember the serene looks on the bottoms' faces. It was more like entering a church than entering a dungeon.

I never wanted to be fisted myself, but because I had small hands and could be quite gentle, I soon became known as an excellent fisting Top. My play in the Catacombs helped accelerate my shift from bottom to Top, and my relationship with George kept evolving. Although he was still the dominant partner in our everyday life, I increasingly became the dominant partner in BDSM play. In the early days of the relationship, George would tie me up and then force his cock into my mouth. As I became a Top, I still loved cock sucking, but the dynamic changed. Now I would tie him up and edge him, allowing him to reach orgasm only when I let him. He loved hoods and gags and surrendered completely when in bondage. Both bondage and fisting freed him psychologically, and he would appear almost angelic when I had my fist in him. I often took control of his breathing, putting my leather-gloved hand over his mouth and nose. He even taught me to make him black out by pushing on his carotid arteries, though I eventually stopped, thinking it too risky. I teased his nipples, beat his balls, and strapped his ass. I loved to get flogged, and George still occasionally topped me, but increasingly I was becoming more his Top than his bottom.

When George suggested that we take a three-week trip to Germany for Oktoberfest in 1977, I jumped at the chance, fulfilling my long-time dream of going to Europe. I had studied German in high school for three years, and I immediately started taking classes in conversational German. George had studied at the Goethe Institute in Germany for over a year. So by the time we left for Europe, I could speak German passably and George was fluent.

Arriving in Frankfurt, we stayed with George's good friends Volker and Norbert. Volker was the road captain of the Frankfurt MSC (Motorcycle Club), and he explained that the major cities in Germany all had motorcycle clubs that formed a network of European leathermen. After getting settled in the apartment, Volker looked at George and suggested that they play. George instantaneously became submissive. They had previously established a comfortable relationship when George had been studying at the Goethe Institute, and George had often bottomed for him. I was very attracted to Norbert, who made it clear through his body language that he wanted me to Top him. I had packed several whips in my bags, including my new mini bullwhip. No one we met in Europe had played with short single tail whips or even seen one before. After flogging Norbert until he was floating, I surprised him by cracking the whip and then using it gently on him.

Both Volker and Norbert had BMW motorcycles, and we explored the area around Frankfurt, with George buddy-riding behind Volker and me behind Norbert. We rode around the countryside in full leathers feeling the cool fall air in our faces, even as we were toasty in our leathers. In the evening we went to the leather bars, where everyone was very welcoming. I was surprised and delighted that the bars had black rooms where leathermen groped one other and had anonymous sex, much like the meat trucks in New York City. After a couple of days of playing and exploring the countryside around Frankfurt, we rode to Munich for Oktoberfest. Together we celebrated the festival in the bars, restaurants, and parks throughout the city, sampling many local craft beers.

In one leather bar we met two extraordinarily good-looking men from Berlin. Michael, an extremely dominant masculine man, was a surgeon. Klaus, a tall handsome leatherman, was a bartender at the Connections, one of the most popular leather bars in Berlin. We enjoyed each other's company, and the six of us hung out together for the next couple of days. George and I had been planning to go to Switzerland when we left Munich, but Michael dissuaded us, saying that Switzerland was boring and we would have a much better time in Berlin staying with them. So after Norbert and Volker headed back to Frankfurt, George and I took a train to join the two men in West Berlin. They met us at the train station. Driving back with them on their motorcycles, I noticed shell marks on the outside walls of their apartment building in the Kreuzberg District of Berlin.

As soon as we entered the apartment, Michael took charge and suggested that we get cleaned up for play. I used the bathroom and returned to the living room to unpack my whips. Klaus returned just a few minutes later. I mentioned the shell marks on the outside of his apartment house. Klaus smiled and said, "Yes, World War II is still quite real to those of us living in Berlin."

George returned from the bathroom, naked except for leather boots and chaps, exposing his cock in front and his bubble butt in back. Michael came into the room, and George immediately knelt down before him. Michael rubbed George's head and asked him if he was ready to get whipped. George nodded and stood up. Michael gently pushed him toward the St. Andrew's Cross. After cuffing him, Michael ran his hands slowly over George's back, whispering something in his ear. Then he began a rhythmic flogging, getting him relaxed and prepared to take a much heavier beating. I loved watching their beautiful dance. George relaxed as Michael steadily flogged the muscles above his shoulder blades. As George started floating, the blows became harder, and he went deeper into subspace. When he began growling, I knew he was feeling his masculine wolf energy with endorphins flowing through him.

At first I found myself identifying with George, but as the play continued I identified more with Michael as Top. I took out my single-tail bullwhip and was holding it in case Michael wanted to use it, but instead Michael indicated that I should take a turn and use it on George. I rose and stood directly behind George. I flicked the whip and lightly grazed him a few times so that I could judge the distance. Then I suddenly cracked the whip in George's ear and allowed the fall to trail slowly down his back. The energy in the room sizzled, and George groaned. After a few more moderate blows with the whip, I nodded and indicated that Michael should finish the scene. Michael kept George in the zone for another ten minutes and then took him off the cross. George kissed his boots, and they fell into each other's arms.

As they held one another, Klaus turned to me and asked me to whip him. I felt the familiar rush from previous experiences topping someone — the thrill of taking control. After flogging his back until it was nicely leathered, I began giving him his first experience with a single tail whip. I was grateful for all the practicing I had done with it before the trip and I had become quite proficient. I think it was at this moment that I began to see myself as a mature leatherman. Klaus bottomed to me beautifully, making me feel completely dominant. I was careful not to crack the whip directly on his back, but instead cracked it above his head and then brought the tip of the tail across his back. Everything in the room receded from my awareness except for Klaus's reactions on the cross: each twitch of his muscles, every sigh and groan. I lost all sense of time and don't know how long I whipped him, but somehow knew that it was time to end. I put down the whip and hugged him. Slowly the room came back into focus and I saw George and Michael staring intensely at me. My eyes connected with George's, and at that moment I knew that everything had changed. I had been topping George fairly regularly before we left for Europe, but he had also been topping me. At this moment I saw my partner as a total bottom, and I think he also saw me then as his Top.

We played all afternoon and well into the evening. It was one of the most intense and satisfying sexual times in my life. At one point I bottomed for Michael, who gave me a wonderful flogging and even tried out my single tail whip on me. He was quite accurate for someone who was using it for the first time. In one very long, memorable scene, George bottomed to all three of us. Everything flowed beautifully. Sex blended perfectly with our BDSM play. We were exhausted when we finally got to bed.

The next day we rode around Berlin and saw the city. Although West Berlin was a very active modern city, rebuilt after the World War II bombing, a wall topped with barbed wire surrounded it. At one point we were able to look over the wall into East Berlin. The sight was quite dismal. Bombed-out buildings were everywhere, and the newly-built apartment houses looked like factories. The people we saw all wore drab gray clothing and walked with their heads down. Michael told us that he and Klaus were prohibited from going to East Berlin, but Americans could get permits to go there for a few hours. Neither George nor I, however, had any interest in visiting such a dismal place, so we declined. Just seeing it from a distance had made quite an impression.

After this unforgettable time in Berlin, we flew to Paris, where we stayed a few days with Gerard. He was George's friend from Alsace, who was a senior officer in the Rothschild Bank in the city. He liked blacking out when he had sex, and I watched George press on his carotid arteries until he passed out. Gerard generously took us to a couple of highly rated restaurants, where I experienced a many-course French meal for the first time in my life. A few days later we were on our way back to America after spending another day with Volker and Norbert in Frankfurt.

Many Americans have reported that their first trip to Europe had somehow changed them. That was also true for me. I now had another vantage point from which to view my life in the United States. I had always been quite passionate about history and had read many books on European history. When I entered buildings that dated back centuries I began to place myself in that history. My sense of self seemed to get more expansive surrounded by the art and architecture from previous centuries. Although on one level everything had seemed quite familiar, there were subtle differences that made me more aware of myself and of my place in the world. I knew enough German that I could usually understand everything, but I had to pay attention to the subtleties of conversations. What had been intuitive for me in the United States now became more self-conscious. I seemed to see things more vividly, realizing the fragility of the bonds between peoples. In Berlin especially, I began to see everything from a fresh vantage point, and life seemed to be more real than anything I had ever experienced before.

My time in Europe made me more introspective about my world and myself. I saw how similar the leather community in Europe was to that in the United States, but subtle differences between the two gave me a new perspective on my experiences, and I began to question my life more explicitly. Why was the leather world so important to me? What was my place in that world? How could I live my life most authentically? After my European trip, these questions framed my life and activities, even though clear answers to them would only emerge gradually over time. I had previously explored whatever life presented, but now I felt a need to pursue an authentic life by taking charge.

The European trip had focused my attention on my leather life by eliminating all other distractions. I wore leather almost constantly, rode on motorcycles with other leathermen, and found respect from others for my whipping skills. Before Europe I had explored the leather world as a way to experience life to the fullest. Now I understood on a deeper level that leathermen were my brothers and I had a responsibility to preserve and guide that community for other explorers. Wearing leather was a badge of honor that had become part of me. Although I would still enjoy bottoming to a few men, I felt more inclined to take charge as a Top. Returning to San Francisco I was now ready to lead my life as a totally committed leatherman.

Chapter 9: WHIPS, WHIPPING, AND THE POWER EXCHANGE

In the early days after our return from Germany, topping George was particularly wonderful. I loved the power that I felt when I controlled him, but I also felt the joy of his surrender. It was a beautiful dance that people now call the power exchange. As he surrendered and went into subspace, I vicariously followed him into the zone. Sometimes in a leather bar, I would find another Top to come back to George's apartment, and we would work him over together.

The Catacombs became one of our most important play spaces. There the serenity of men dressed in leather created a great environment for BDSM. The European trip had empowered me as a Top, and the Catacombs now reinforced a sense of myself as dominant. Although the Catacombs were legendary throughout the world for fisting, other BDSM activities took place there as well. Guys who wanted a fisting Top often sought me out, but so did those who wanted a good whipping.

Although George and I continued to play together into the 1980s, our relationship as partners ended in 1978, when he met a cute young boy named Jeffrey. I again started spending more time at my home with Don. We never had a monogamous relationship; I was just happy to be a part of Don's life and was never jealous. He has been my closest friend, and we have always looked out for each other. Don had met a new partner, Michael Spitznagel, who had moved into our apartment on Noe Street. It became quite cramped, however, when I started spending more time there, so the three of us moved into a more spacious place on Church Street and 21st that had an upstairs flat and a large room in the basement with high ceilings — a perfect place for a dungeon. It was the first time we'd had space for a dedicated playroom.

Don and I had paying jobs, but Michael needed a way to earn an income. He thought we could make some money by becoming professional leather Doms, and we put an ad in the *Bay Area Reporter* that said, "$75 for scenes to fulfill your BDSM fantasies with hot leathermen. Dungeon and Masters available." We opened our own dungeon and became sex workers. Almost all of the guys who became our clients were bottoms, and we got lots of calls. Whips were on the wall — mostly from my collection. There was a spanking bench, a cross, and a bondage bed.

We asked our clients to tell us about their fantasies. Some guys were very articulate, but with others we experimented through trial and error. We learned to get information on the phone and often had a good idea of what to do before a guy even came into the house. Once we knew what someone wanted, one of us would lead him into the basement. Most of the men had a good time, and there were a lot of repeats, which made it even easier to arrange scenes. We always asked whether our clients minded marks and bruises. Since so many men were married and closeted, we often had to be careful. For masochists who did not want marks, tit clamps, Wartenberg wheels, and clothespins could give a lot of pain and pleasure. We were all good with whips, though each of us had other specialties as well.

Depriving guys of sight often heightened their experiences, but we always asked if they were claustrophobic before putting on blindfolds or hoods. Most guys loved being gagged. We experimented with music, but found that silence and a subdued atmosphere were usually more effective. After a few weeks we intuitively knew how to maximize the anticipation and create psychological excitement. I remember a lot of guys trembling as they went down the stairs. That usually signaled that the scene would be successful and probably lead to repeat business.

Michael was a good-looking, six-foot-four-inch man and mostly a Top, bottoming only with Don. He loved BDSM play and was very creative. The dungeon was really his business venture, and he had a lot of clients during the week while Don and I were working. We would, however, join him on the weekends when he needed help. Michael was very good at sex scenes. He had a big cock and liked to use it. He would make guys suck him, and he liked fucking guys who wanted that. The sex was always in the context of BDSM, however, and he would bark out orders, since most wanted a dominant man. Michael would chat with a guy just long enough to find out what he was looking for. Then he took control and led him into the basement.

The clients often quivered when we made them strip before a "Master" wearing leather. Although they were often embarrassed, their dicks usually got hard when we stripped them, creating even deeper submissive feelings. Michael was very good at playing on this excitement, getting them to surrender and submit even more. Staring at them, he would quietly tell them to kneel and put their hands behind their backs or behind their necks. He would have them spread their legs apart as he played with their dicks and squeezed their balls.

One Saturday a tall, blond, well-spoken Englishman (also named Michael) came and wanted to be caned. I was elected because I enjoyed caning guys. He didn't give me any clues about how he wanted it, so I made it up. I told him, "You're going to polish these riding boots." When he finished polishing the boots, I intended to find something unacceptable and give him a caning with a certain number of strokes. "You have one hour to polish these boots. Here are the polish, rags, and all the material you need in this boot kit." I went upstairs. When I returned I saw that the guy had barely touched the boots. I was dressed in leather and he was naked. I put my hand on his shoulder and looked him in the eye, "What have you been doing for an hour? Don't you know how to polish boots? You're British. You ought to know how to polish these fucking boots." He said, "Well, they're colonial boots and not proper English ones. They're impossible to polish." I immediately said, "You'll pay the price for your impudence and insubordination. Get over this bench now." He hesitated for a second, but then complied as I looked at him without wavering. Totally consumed in playing the Master, I determined that he would get a severe caning. Since that's what he wanted, he wasn't disappointed. He cried out a few times for mercy, but I mostly ignored him, though I slowed down the pace a little.

Then, I decided I'd end it with a game. I said, "You're not in England and are being so disrespectful of us colonials. Where do you think you are?" He looked bewildered and I immediately said, "You're in San Francisco."

"I know that," he smirked.

"Well," I said, "we're going to see if you know how to spell San Francisco." With every letter I gave him a hard blow of the cane. He got so excited by the caning that he couldn't spell it. Several times he got to F-R-A-N and then said "S." And we started over. I don't know to this day whether he was doing it on purpose or was truly flustered. I don't remember how many times we started over, but eventually he got the letters right and put a "C" after F-R-A-N. That was perhaps the hardest caning I've ever given. I had marked him badly, and his ass was covered in welts, with a little bleeding. We both had a very good time, however, and this was clearly what he had wanted.

We so enjoyed our BDSM play that I invited him to come back and stay at our place the next time he could get back to San Francisco. A couple of months later he stayed with us for two weeks. He knew just how to bring out my Dominance. A day after he arrived, we were walking back to the house after a Saturday brunch in a diner, when he turned toward me and asked whether I knew anyone who was man enough to give him a proper whipping. He cocked his head and looked impishly at me.

"I'll give you a whipping that you'll remember for quite a while," I responded.

He smiled and said, "I've only found a couple of men who could keep such a promise, but you can try."

Sexual excitement matched my sudden determination to take control. A few minutes later we entered the apartment and I told him to use the bathroom and I'd see him in the dungeon in fifteen minutes. He inclined his head and said quietly, "Yes Sir." Like a lot of guys who can take a severe ass beating, he was much more sensitive to pain on his back, so I didn't have to flog him very long before I felt his surrender. While he could take a very heavy caning, he hadn't had much experience being whipped on the back. I gently rubbed his shoulders and asked, "You do want to please me, don't you? How many strokes will you take from my single-tail whip?"

"Eight, Sir," he softly replied. From his slight hesitation, I knew that he believed he was setting a high bar for himself.

"You'll take ten," I said, feeling it important to stay in control. I made a show of cracking the whip, but in the end gave him fairly light strokes. It's important for a Top to judge the experience level of the bottom. I had already learned that it's best to start light and slowly get heavier as the bottom gains more trust and confidence in his ability to absorb the pain. When I finished, Michael was floating. The Dominant/submissive bond we had forged in this early scene lasted for the rest of his visit, though he knew he could easily get my attention by becoming a little sassy. He had learned that combining submission with a little impudence would instantly fire up my Dominance. By the end of his stay, we had established a deep friendship that has lasted until today. I have visited him several times in England. And, of course, when I was there he had no trouble convincing me to give him a good caning.

Our dungeon on Church Street came to an abrupt end in late 1979. A guy came to the dungeon during the week and told our roommate Michael that his fantasy was to be used by a Master in any way he wanted to use him. So Michael created a scene to use the guy just as he wanted. Even as the scene developed, Michael could tell that things weren't going too well. But he was unprepared for the guy's response when the scene ended. "I got nothing out of that experience. You didn't give me any satisfaction." Michael had invested a lot of time trying to make the scene work and did just what the man asked — to use him any way he wanted. So Michael refused to give him back the seventy-five dollars.

Then the anonymous calls began. Police would wake us up late at night, saying that they had calls of someone in distress at our address. Or the fire department would respond to a call at 3:00 a.m. and the whole apartment house would be evacuated. We could never prove who had made those calls, but it was almost certainly the guy who claimed that he had a bad scene in our dungeon. Our landlord had known what we were doing, but now told us we would have to leave the apartment, because it was disrupting too many other people in the building.

I've known other people who have tried to become sex workers doing BDSM scenes. It often works for a while, but something almost always happens to end the business abruptly. When guys pay for sex, they don't fully entrust power to the Top, but actually control the scene. Men pay for sex to create their fantasies. Since they have paid for a particular fantasy the "Master" actually becomes more of a service Top, giving clients what they want, rather than truly being in charge.

Despite this, I learned a lot about topping in our dungeon on Church Street and began to understand why some scenes were more successful than others. When the bottom could clearly tell us what he wanted we were generally more successful. What physical activities did they want? What intensity level? The bottom would often drop clues about what they were psychologically looking for as well.

I often conducted the initial discussion in the dungeon itself. The whips were all on the wall, and I'd have the guys choose the whips they wanted me to use. I asked whether they wanted their asses played with and opened a drawer and gave them a choice of dildos. I'd let them choose gags, blindfolds, and hoods. I always thought of sex as a banquet, and I let the guys order their meals. Of course, I supplied the psychological spice that made the banquet interesting.

Most bottoms wanted a Top to take control and be assertive, but sometimes we had to guess whether a man needed to be humbled by licking boots or praised for being a strong man who could take what we were giving. Many guys did not have a lot of experience and only gave us very general guidelines. The more I played, however, the better I became at reading a bottom's reactions and making adjustments while the scene was happening. How did the bottom react physically to the intensity of an activity? Was the guy compliant or did he resist? Did he look directly at me or keep his eyes averted? I not only had to watch carefully, but also had to interpret the meaning behind his reactions. Was he role-playing or was the reaction genuine? Luckily I have always been intuitive and usually knew what I needed to do. There was, of course, a lot of trial and error. I would try something, but quickly back away from it and do something else if it wasn't working.

I was most successful when the bottom opened himself up to the experience; then I could feel myself empathetically opening up as well — almost thinking the same thoughts and even feeling the same pain. A good Top can create a connection by a touch or by a word of encouragement. Telling a bottom to let go or relax at the right moment can be quite powerful, just as touching him in certain ways can create various moods. But the bottom also communicates his experience by his movements, sighs, laughter, cries, and other general responses. Both Top and bottom must communicate verbally before a scene and non-verbally during it. In retrospect, the timing was right for closing our dungeon. I had learned a lot, but it was time to move on.

There was only one time that I remember any of us taking the role of bottom in our professional dungeon. A leatherman, known as "Dick the Cop," came over and pulled out seventy-five dollars and said he wanted a slave. I've always had a huge fetish for being topped by a cop, so I volunteered. He was in magnificent shape, a six-foot-four-inch, dark-haired, muscular guy with blue eyes, almost like a statue of a Greek god, and he rode a motorcycle. I was disappointed that he would never wear his police uniform to play, though he always wore lots of leather — boots, harnesses, chaps, leather shirts, etc. He gave me such a wonderful whipping that day that I gave him back his seventy-five dollars.

Later, we got to know each other quite well in the leather world. I was thrilled whenever he wanted to use me. A couple of years later we both attended Inferno, an annual leather encampment organized by the Chicago Hellfire Club, the first gay men's BDSM club in the nation. Dick was one of the few guys who could throw a bullwhip with precision, so I asked him to fulfill one of my fantasies, and he agreed. I wanted 300 hard strokes with his eight-foot bullwhip — as hard as he could. He was not only extremely precise, but he was also quite theatrical. He cracked the bullwhip right near my ear and then hit a precise spot of the back. He had worked at Universal Studios for a while as a stunt man in their *Wild West Show* and was one of the best whip throwers I have ever met, if not the very best.

At Inferno, he shackled me to a St. Andrew's Cross and put a football helmet on my head. He teased me by cracking the whip around my head until the sound alone almost drove me into subspace. Then he methodically began cutting my back and butt with 300 strokes. I was a bloody mess when he ended, but I was never so high on endorphins. I am glad that I got to experience such an extreme whipping once in my life, something I had fantasized about since I was a young boy. He took me to a place of absolute abandon, a beautiful place where I floated in ecstasy for many hours. The body would heal in a few months, but I had experienced something truly transcendental. I went home on an airplane the next day and bled through my t-shirt, my regular shirt, and a light jacket onto the airline seat. I sneaked into the bathroom and got paper towels and soap to clean the seat where I had bled through before anyone noticed. Luckily it was nighttime, and the seat next to me was empty.

Why do we do these things? Why do I feel the need to whip someone, just as I sometimes feel the need to be whipped? For me the play is sensual, sexual, and even sacred. A mysterious connection beyond words can occur between the two men in BDSM play. There is also something extremely masculine about both whipping and getting whipped. When I whip others, I feel an energy travel through my body, down my arm, and into the whip; when the whip strikes the back of a man who is offering himself to me, I feel a thrilling connection with him.

The physical act of getting whipped is pleasurable in itself because it releases endorphins. But it goes beyond that. When I've been whipped I am incredibly close to the man who whipped me, and I feel free. Like most spiritual experiences this one will seem bizarre unless it has been experienced. Words fail. There is a unity which is not just between the two men, but which begins to encompass the universe itself. The burdens of life melt away and there is pure joy. That's why I play with whips — and I think that's why many others play with whips as well.

The catharsis that often occurs during the flogging becomes quite intense when I take a thoroughly-whipped man down from a St. Andrew's Cross and then hug him and hold him in my arms. Sometimes there are tears, sometimes laughter, but almost always a sense of freedom and deep gratitude. I share in that experience also as the Top. I feel a deep caring for the man I've just whipped.

I once had a scene at Inferno with a muscular, handsome man named Fred. He began to use his six-foot bullwhip on me. He would crack the whip and I'd feel an instant of pain that would then transform into an exhilarating energy that I perceived as both sexual and spiritual. As the whipping continued, the energy overwhelmed and engulfed me. We were involved in some kind of mysterious dance. Waves of orgasmic pleasure coursed through my body. I felt myself floating outside my body, and I simultaneously became a small intimate part of the universe that expanded until I felt myself encompassing all of existence. It was so extraordinary, because I was both entirely in the scene, yet was watching the scene from above at the same time.

I assume that Fred was also feeling a similar spiritual ecstasy. I certainly get as high when I'm topping as when I've bottomed. That's the wonderful thing about the dance that takes place in a powerful whipping scene — the man throwing the whip gives ecstasy to the man receiving it, but simultaneously experiences the beauty of the trust and abandon that the whipped man gives him. It's a journey that Top and bottom take together. Both go into a blissful state together or they don't get there at all. If the scene is profound for one of them, it is almost always profound for the other as well. If one man is high, then so is the other. The two men are joined together in the experience. That's now called the "power exchange" and is central to whipping and all other forms of BDSM play. If the two men don't establish a connection at the beginning, then the scene won't work at all. Both men go through the "doors of perception" together, to borrow an expression from Aldous Huxley.

I not only love the experience of whipping and being whipped, but I am also passionate about my whip collection. I have now collected over 1000 whips from all over the world, and I have used each one of them in play. I am fascinated with how various whips from different countries were made and how they were originally used. I started going to flea markets and auctions just to find whips. They have become my holy objects, and I get high from handling, smelling, and oiling them. Each whip has a story associated with it. They are for me like the holy scourges associated with the lives of the saints. When I use the whips in dungeon play they become sacred implements that can open up deep spiritual realities both for the man I'm playing with and for me.

The oldest of my whips is almost 200 years old. I got it from a man I played with in 1969 in New York. It was a legacy from his family plantation; I traded him for some rare porn. Made between 1830 and 1840, it was used to whip slaves in Alabama. At first I didn't want to use it, because it had originally been used to brutalize black men and women in perpetuating slavery. But after reflection I decided it was all right to use the whip consensually to create pleasure and form a caring bond between two men. It is an Argentine-style whip and really doesn't leave heavy marks. It has aged well and will probably last another couple of hundred years. The other old whip came from the Brook family plantation that was near my own ancestors' 640-acre tobacco plantation in Maryland. I bought this whip, with its decorative motif of tobacco leaves, in an auction. It was a lady's ivory riding crop with cloth and silk from about 1840. I still use it as well.

As I use whips, I imagine the lives of the men who had used them to herd cattle, drive stagecoaches, or star in rodeo shows. Through them I get to know many diverse cultures throughout the world, especially their arts and crafts. These whips now also embody the lives of all the men I've played with and all the scenes of which I've been a part. Rituals have evolved. I will often lay some whips out on a table or a bed and tell a little story about each. And then I will ask a man which whips he would like to experience. Together, we then become part of a spiritual brotherhood with the other men who have experienced the pain and pleasure of a cathartic whipping.

Whips for me are as special as surgical instruments are for a surgeon. A good Top has to know how to use them accurately and skillfully. He has to read the bottom's reaction to each stroke and evaluate the intensity, the frequency, and the area of impact. He has to be skilled in cracking a whip and precise about where the blow lands. A skilled Top learns to create the psychological context as well. That can be done with pacing, touch, encouragement, and words. A good bottom also realizes that he is a co-partner in creating a successful scene. He will focus all his attention on the scene and react honestly to the whip.

When we were forced to leave our apartment at Church and 21st, I decided that it was time for me to take an apartment of my own. Don and Michael were partners; George had taken up with Jeffrey, a young man who was beginning to explore the leather world. I leased a two-bedroom apartment by myself and used one bedroom for sleeping and the other for my rather large collection of whips. Now that our dungeon had closed, I could focus all my attention on bonding with the men I whipped. Only a couple of months after taking my new apartment six men formed the first gay leatherman's BDSM club in San Francisco. Although not one of the original six founders, I was the first member to join The 15 Association when it formed. From that time until today, forging a strong leather brotherhood would become a central part of my leather life.

Chapter 10: A LEATHER BROTHERHOOD

In the fall of 1978 I met one of the most inspiring men in my life, a man who crystallized for me the importance of the leather community as a brotherhood of men who supported one another. I had been invited to a private party of leathermen who were welcoming Felix Jones to San Francisco. Felix had been instrumental in founding the European leather scene in the 1950s, and in 1965, along with Tony Hepworth, was the co-founder of the Sixty Nine Club (SNC), a motorcycle group in London.

After dinner, the guest of honor seemed to single me out for conversation, and we ended up talking for over an hour. Felix and I had an immediate rapport, although he was thirty years older. His sheer presence and magnetic personality drew people into his orbit. He asked me about my experiences in the leather community, and I told him about coming to San Francisco to become a leatherman, riding motorcycles to leather runs, and becoming a member of the Koalas. He was particularly interested in hearing about my whip collection and how I used them in BDSM play. I learned that he shared my passion for the history of flagellation in the British military. Like me, he loved whips, flogging, and men in uniform.

Felix was a wonderful storyteller and needed little encouragement to talk about the beginning of the gay men's motorcycle clubs after World War II. I mentioned that I had briefly met him in 1971, when he and other European bikers were on tour in America. He shared details of the trip and told me how much he loved touring the East Coast with his European friends. When he saw my interest in history, particularly English military history, he recounted enlisting in the British Army when war broke out in 1939 and serving under General Montgomery in North Africa and Italy. Soon he was talking about spending furloughs in Cairo with "dear Noel," his lifelong friend. "Dear Noel" turned out to be Noel Coward, the famous playwright and actor who at that time had been working for the Secret Service.

I was so enchanted by Felix's stories that I could have listened for hours, but he realized that he needed to circulate among others at the party and eventually excused himself. When he left me, he said that I should visit him in London sometime soon, and I replied that I was planning a trip there in a few months.

A couple of weeks after the social gathering for Felix in San Francisco I received a warm letter from John and Bernie, two English leathermen, inviting me to stay with them in London. I had found their names in *Drummer* magazine and had sent a letter to ask whether I could visit them. They wrote that I would be very welcome, and suggested that I come for a couple of weeks sometime in January. In those days, leathermen customarily invited others visiting their cities to stay with them. Don, Michael, and I often had visiting leathermen staying with us on Church Street.

It was bitter cold when I arrived in London on New Year's Eve of 1978-79. The temperature never went above freezing during the first week I was there, and snow covered the ground. Yet the reception from John and Bernie was exceedingly warm as they helped me plan my stay in London. A couple of days after I got settled, they invited some friends in the leather community over to their house to meet me.

Felix Jones was among the twenty leather guys who arrived after dinner a few days later. He insisted on seeing the whips I had brought over and was particularly impressed by the single tail whips made by David Morgan. The slave whip interested him greatly, and he told me that he wanted to experience it before I left England. I also showed him one of my British cat-o'-nine-tails that had once been used for punishment in the Royal Navy. It was an extremely well made whip and had become one of my favorites. That evening Felix was the center of attention as he told stories about his World War II experiences.

That night Felix admitted that he had arranged for me to be at his welcoming party in San Francisco so that he could check me out before his friends agreed to host me. He laughed, saying that I had obviously passed the test. I learned that Felix was a professional butler who worked for members of the royal family in England, occasionally substituting as butler for the Queen, the Queen Mother, and Princess Margaret. When he learned of my interest in English royalty, he told me to write the Queen Mother and ask her to become my surrogate grandmother; my own grandmother had been very important to me, but died in my youth. I was thrilled when the Queen Mother wrote back, saying that she would be happy to be my honorary grandmother. A few years later I had a personal audience with her and together we drank a generous portion of the fine gin I had brought as a gift.

Felix and I shared so much in common. Early in our youth we had both become interested in the leather world and shared whipping and uniforms as our main fetishes. We loved the company of men and shared a zest for hard play at parties. He had a booming voice and military bearing that made him a gigantic presence at any social event, even though he was shorter than I, only four feet eleven inches tall. He would become quite theatrical when he told his stories, imitating the speech and body posture of various characters. At the twenty-fifth Anniversary Weekend of the Sixty Nine Club in 1990, for example, he entertained everyone throughout the evening by playing the roles of a baby, Queen Victoria, and an old man.

Over the next couple of years, Felix and I became close friends. He introduced me to many men who have become icons of the leather world. That summer when I stayed with him in London, he took me to the leather shop run by his friend Alan Selby, who would immigrate to San Francisco a few months later and open the famous Mr. S Leather store. Eventually he became affectionately known as the "Mayor of Folsom Street." Back in 1971, Felix and Alan had founded the first gay rubber club in Europe (RMC). Alan became a very good friend after moving to San Francisco. Through Felix I would also meet Tom of Finland (Touko Laaksonen) who would stay with Felix when visiting London. In the fall of 1980 I flew to New York City to hang out with Felix and Tom, attending together the Fall Review of the American Uniform Association (AUA). What a week! I watched Tom make sketches of men in uniform at AUA events. The three of us attended parties throughout the city. We played at the Mineshaft and then ended up going to Wally Wallace's infamous parties at his Loft. Wally was the owner of the Mineshaft. At the party, I saw a man on all fours taking pictures of men's boots and crotches. I smiled when I realized it was Tom of Finland.

Felix not only became one of my closest friends, he also became a mentor who taught me the importance of organized leather groups. One day in the summer of 1979, while I was staying with him in London, he listed all the leather groups he had helped organize in Europe. While he was telling me the story of founding the European Confederation of Motorcycle Clubs (ECMC) to coordinate the activities of thirty-five clubs throughout Europe, he became pensive and said, "Peter, we can play and enjoy ourselves as we wish, only because we have these robust leather organizations for support."

The conversation then turned even more sober as we talked about the wild excesses of drugs and careless SM play occurring in the late 1970s. I told him about a party I had attended at Hank Diethelm's house in 1978 that had been haunting me ever since. Hank had a large house with a huge basement dungeon with two prison cells, a large dog cage, several St. Andrew's Crosses, bondage tables, slings, and even a coffin. There was a shower large enough for at least six men. Munchies, including marijuana brownies, were on tables, along with bowls of cocaine, mescaline, and speed. Some folks were using needles to shoot up. Men were having wild sex throughout the house, not only on the main floor but also upstairs and in the attic.

At about 2:00 a.m. I had finished a couple of whipping scenes and was just hanging out in the dungeon, talking with Hank, while watching a medical scene develop. Four men were topping two bottoms, strapped to adjoining tables. They began with a slow inspection of all parts of the "patients'" bodies — fingers probing into anal and oral cavities. Thermometers were inserted into the guys' asses, their balls were squeezed and palpitated. One Top meticulously shaved all parts of the boys' bodies using a straight razor. Then someone applied a dark yellow disinfectant. Sterile needles were inserted through the nipples of one guy and through the cock head of another in a pattern known as a "crown of thorns." They began playing with Exacto knives, cutting the pectoral areas of the chest and stomach. Blood began flowing. When one guy started cutting on a boy's scrotum, both Hank and I decided we'd had enough. I'd seen many BDSM scenes, but this was beyond any SM play that I wanted to see.

Hank and I made our way upstairs from the basement. We stepped over the bodies of guys who had taken too many drugs. Others were fucking on couches and on the rug in the middle of the floor. We finally got to Hank's bedroom on the second floor, and he said, "I'm glad I locked the door before the party or there would be guys sprawled out in here too." Hank vowed that he would only have close friends over in the future. "I don't know half the guys here tonight. I just hope that no one overdoses or gets hurt." As we cuddled and fell asleep, I reflected on how the leather scene had changed since my early days in San Francisco.

Felix had listened to my story without interrupting. He now put into words what had been bothering me. "I started a motorcycle club in England because I wanted to find the same masculine companionship and solidarity that I had found in the military. We were brothers and had each other's backs. I fought next to men of honor and courage, some of them gay. We rode motorcycles and played hard because we trusted one another. We are first and foremost a gay brotherhood. It seems that many blokes now just want to have a good time without feeling any responsibility for anyone else."

"I think the drug culture is partly to blame," I responded. "Let me tell you something that happened a few months ago that I'm not proud of. I met a man who was a very skilled whip thrower, and we went to the South of the Slot Hotel, a place where guys take rooms for fisting and BDSM play. The Slot is also notorious for its drug use. We both got extremely high on mescaline and then went to the roof to play. I took off my shirt and told him to give me a good whipping. To make a long story short, he had barely begun, when the whip hit the side of my face leaving an inch-long welt halfway between my ear and my eye. I almost lost that eye. I will never play again when either of us has taken drugs or drunk more than a beer. I'm not proud that I was so irresponsible."

Felix gazed at me and lowered his voice, "This cannot go on. It's just too wild. We're losing our sense of fellowship and joy. Something bad is going to happen. We played hard and drank our share of beer. But we took care of one another. When someone drank too much, his leather brothers watched out for him." He paused and I thought back to my days riding with Billy on the motorcycle runs. Then he said, quite dramatically, "Peter, that's why it's so important to have leather organizations that foster brotherhood and keep us from doing something too crazy. When all is said and done, we'll remember the friendships more than the wild scenes."

My conversations with Felix made me realize that I longed for a brotherhood of gay men who were into SM play. A few months earlier, I had briefly become involved with a group of men who tried to form such a club. A group of Tops had organized some play parties, but they met secretly to decide policies. Although I was a switch and increasingly played more as a Top, I was still seen as a bottom in the leather world. So I waited with the other bottoms in the basement for the play to begin, while the Tops met upstairs. After the third or fourth party, we bottoms rebelled and simply walked out, disgusted by the secrecy and lack of respect. I still yearned, however, for an organization that would be a true brotherhood for all gay men interested in SM.

In February 1980, approximately six months after my conversation with Felix, six men met to register a new non-profit organization with the State of California. They called the organization "The 15 Association." They printed a poster with "The 15" logo that is used to this day. The poster set out its ideals for the community. They would be "a group of men who will stick together as buddies, providing each other with mutual support and friendship." They were "A Leather-S&M/B&D Fraternity" that would hold "parties and events exclusively for ourselves and our invited guests." As "an elite corps ... highly visible" they would "interface with the open gay community to promote a positive image of gay S&M and leather scenes."

Three of the six founders had just attended Inferno VIII, a long weekend of heavy SM play that was organized by Chicago Hellfire, the oldest gay BDSM club in the United States. These three men had enjoyed the heavy play and fellowship at Inferno so much that they asked the Chicago group to organize a West Coast branch but were told to start their own group. Alexis Sorel, one of the three at Inferno, had also been an early member of the Society of Janus, a pansexual BDSM educational and support group in San Francisco that had occasional play parties. Janus was primarily a heterosexual group, though a few gay men and lesbians belonged.

The six founders of The 15 would model the new organization after Hellfire. A group of Fraternals would form the center of the organization, doing the work and voting on policies. This core group would be limited to no more than fifteen men, to keep it from becoming unwieldy. Others could join as Associate members. At the beginning only Tops could be Fraternals, though anyone could attend meetings and voice their opinions and help make decisions. Interestingly, two of the six founders were bottoms and therefore could not become Fraternals or have a vote, but less than a year later that policy was changed.

Sometime in early May, Alexis Sorel called and told me about his mind-blowing experience at Inferno VIII. Then he said, "A few of us are forming a similar group here in San Francisco to organize SM play parties. You'll see an announcement in the *Bay Area Reporter* in a few days, and I know you'll be interested. We're looking for guys to join. It's going to be like the bike clubs, a brotherhood where members support one another. You should become a member."

I told him about my experience with the guys who tried to form such a club, while excluding bottoms from the discussions and meetings.

"You know me, Peter. I don't like secrecy. Our meetings are completely open, and anyone can voice his point of view. Two of the six men who are creating our group — Chump and Jerry Jansen — are total bottoms. You know both of them well."

"Then count me in. Where do I sign up?" I liked the idea of a men-only club that was organized like the bike clubs, but dedicated to SM play.

He told me that they were having interviews for members in a couple of days at the 527, a leather bar and restaurant on Bryant Street. I arrived early and was first in a line of about ten guys when Alexis opened the door and ushered me into a private room where the other founders of The 15 Association were waiting.

I knew four of the men in the room really well, Alexis best of all. He was from Colombia and liked to say that he was born in the shadow of a volcano. We frequently played together, and I counted him among my best friends. Although Alexis told everyone he was a Top, he was actually a switch, or at least he was when he played with me. When we got together to play, we would decide on the spot who would be Top and who would be bottom. By 1980 the word "switch" was beginning to be used in leather circles and the concept was no longer quite as alien as it had been a few years before.

Alexis was one of the most adventurous and open leathermen that I've known. I respected his proficiency in throwing a whip, and he equally loved to be whipped. Our play was often experimental. I remember one time when we beat each other's asses with the flat side of machetes and experimented with cutting scenes. He was one of the first men to begin leather play at Radical Faerie gatherings, becoming part of a group known informally as "black leather wings." The Radical Faeries formed in 1979 as a countercultural gay group to resist the norms of heterosexual society and celebrate a queer sexuality. Most resisted capitalism and encouraged ecological awareness.

I also knew Jerry Jansen, Alexis's partner, well. He was a total bottom and often sought me out to give him a good birching or caning. Jerry is the only founder of The 15 who is still alive. Although he is no longer a member, he still occasionally comes to our parties. David Lewis and his boy, Jim Lansdown, known by everyone as "Chump," were also good friends. They had attended Inferno VIII with Alexis and, like him, returned bursting with enthusiasm. David shared my passion for whips and played hard. We frequently discussed various styles of whips and the best whip makers in the United States. Actually, all six of the founders were fond of impact play, especially whipping. Many gay bikers would refer to The 15 disparagingly as "the whipping club."

I didn't know the other two men as well. Dick Kaufman was an older man, then in his sixties. He had been a member of the Satyrs and I had met and played with him once at a Satyrs run, but only knew him as a casual acquaintance. I got to know Roy Richard only later as a club member. He was a big, bulky, muscular blacksmith, who had moved to San Francisco from Pennsylvania.

When I entered the private room at the back of the restaurant, Alexis introduced me and asked why I wanted to join. I explained that I had moved to San Francisco to become a leatherman after reading the articles in *Life* magazine. I had

A Leather Brotherhood

been a member of the Koalas and had attended many of the bike runs, where I had discovered a leather brotherhood. I said that I loved whips and whipping and wanted to promote safe BDSM play. After less than five minutes, Alexis interrupted me, "You know four of us well and we have played with you." He looked at the other two, who nodded. He then turned to me and said, "You're in. Send the next person into the room." By the end of the day fifteen or sixteen men had joined the club as founding members. The 15 Association thus became a viable gay men's SM brotherhood — the first on the West Coast and the second in the nation.

We spent the next few weeks discussing plans for our first play party. Although only the Fraternal members of The 15 could vote, all of us seemed to be on the same page and there weren't any controversies. We decided to begin looking for our own clubhouse, so that we could have monthly BDSM parties. In the meantime we looked for a temporary place to play. We rented a dungeon space at Army and Mission owned by a lesbian couple who made their money as Pro-Dommes, charging straight men for BDSM sessions. We called our first play parties "scenes"; they became "15 play parties" after we got our clubhouse. Scene I took place on June 16, my thrity-fifth birthday, and I celebrated with an intense whipping. We were surprised that the first party drew about seventy guys, and were even more delighted that half of them became members.

We held four scenes before we opened our own clubhouse in the SOMA district on Ritch Street in January 1981 and began holding monthly parties in the basement dungeon. The main floor had a kitchen and lounge area, and Roy Richards and his partner lived upstairs. The first party at our clubhouse was packed since we had grown to over 150 members. We arranged for the Police and Fire Commissioner to inspect the place. We were surprised that six of the eleven

San Francisco Supervisors had accepted our invitation to see the clubhouse a couple of days before. Three of the Supervisors actually showed up for the party itself. I was standing nearby when one of the Fraternals tactfully suggested that the woman Supervisor enjoy the refreshments in the lounge area, since the play had already begun downstairs. The two male Supervisors went down to watch for a few minutes.

Almost every conceivable BDSM activity took place at these first parties in our clubhouse. The most popular activity of The 15 Association has always been impact play, whipping on St. Andrew's Crosses, caning on spanking benches, and an occasional punching scene. But we also had slings for fisting and a tub in a corner for piss play. One guy even brought his own rim seat. And there was lots of sex. After a good BDSM scene the bottom often got on his knees, thanking the Top by sucking his cock. Ass play and fucking were common, and in those days we didn't use condoms.

To some degree, we were all voyeurs and exhibitionists or we wouldn't have been playing in an open space. Everyone watched, and everyone knew we were being watched. Both Tops and bottoms wanted to become known as skilled players. Although most guys at the parties were known as either Tops or bottoms, I switched roles, and my specialty was whipping and being whipped. I spent time at home practicing with the whips I had collected from around the world. I also knew to adjust the intensity to match a bottom's experience and body type. When I bottomed, I totally submitted both my body and my mind to the guy whipping me. That required me to be somewhat selective, since I needed to trust a Top before I could surrender.

Leathermen spent considerable thought on the aesthetics of play. One guy painstakingly painted wooden clothespins various colors so he could arrange them artfully on a bottom's balls, cock, inner thighs, and chest. Tops knew that others were judging their skills in tying good-looking and secure knots when they bound someone to a table. We all watched when someone brought a new activity to a party. Even though I never cared to develop skill at electric play, I was fascinated when I first saw someone playing with a TENS unit.

Watching others play wasn't just entertainment: it was an education that made us all better players. We watched Tops play so we could become better Tops. We watched bottoms play to authenticate their masculinity, while we admired their trust and surrender. Many BDSM groups teach skills, safety, and information through demonstrations and talks by leaders in the community. The 15 Association has held its share of such events. However, the prime way that gay men learn about BDSM is through watching other men play. Through observation one learns different styles. In our social space, men shared information with each other. Occasionally a new person would approach someone known for his skills and ask to be mentored. Now when someone asks me how to get into BDSM play, I suggest that they go to play parties of organized groups. They are not only the safest places to begin playing, but they are also settings to learn about safe, sane, and consensual play.

From the very beginning, The 15 Association has always taken safety precautions seriously, while at the same time allowing men to engage in mutually agreed-upon heavy and intense play. Many early discussions at the meetings of The 15 Association were about facilitating safe and consensual play without unduly interfering with scenes. We made sure that all the equipment at our clubhouse was well constructed, and the Fraternals took charge of designating monitors to oversee dungeon play.

When we formed The 15 Association, the leather bikers were quite critical. They didn't like our linking leather with BDSM. It was fine if leathermen did BDSM privately, but they objected to our openly advertising for members. I have never liked gay men to criticize as rash those who are more adventurous, while at the same time criticizing other gays for not being masculine enough. Some gay men wished that we'd go away, because they were trying to blend into the norms of the straight world, with the exception of their sexual preference. We basically ignored all these criticisms, openly advertising our events in the *Bay Area Reporter*, thereby carving out a space for those of us who found our sexual attraction to other men entwined with our interests in BDSM.

Just about the time we opened our dungeon and clubhouse, gay men began getting sick from a mysterious disease. By the spring of 1982, a large number of our members got terribly sick, and things fell apart. The first sign was lesions, then the victim became weak, wasted away, and usually died within six months. Doctors identified the disease as a very rare form of cancer known as Kaposi's Sarcoma. But why was it spreading, and why did it seem to primarily attack gay men? It wasn't until 1983 that doctors identified the disease as the HIV retrovirus spread by sex and needles. By that time San Francisco General Hospital had a special ward for men who were dying of the disease. Although the health care workers at SF General were kind, they took extreme precautions to isolate the patients, who often died without any human touch.

In the spring of 1982, however, no one knew how the disease was spreading, and there were even rumors that the government was poisoning gay men. Members of The 15 Association were hit hard. Compassion for our sick brothers struggled with fear. Even today it is painful to reflect on this dreadful time. As horrific as it was, I feel considerable pride in how my brothers responded to the crisis. Since the disease was hitting all segments of the gay community, most guys set aside their differences, and leathermen began working beside drag queens to raise money for the Godfather Fund to help men stricken by the disease. Our members regularly visited patients in the AIDS ward at SF General. Some of our lesbian friends were truly heroic, providing human contact to dying gay men. I forced myself to visit these men in the hospital, and afterwards found myself terribly depressed.

Alan Selby began organizing fundraisers, and I immediately jumped in to help. In September 1983 I helped him organize the San Francisco Leather Daddy's boy contest that raised considerable money for the AIDS Emergency Fund. I was much better at raising funds than visiting the sick. Coulter "Colt" Thomas had come to San Francisco with his partner Charlie to be one of the judges at the contest. Only four months earlier, he had won the fifth International Mr. Leather contest in Chicago. Working with him and others putting on the San Francisco event was paradoxically a joyous day. When his partner Charlie died of AIDS, Coulter became my partner and the love of my life until he himself died of AIDS in 1992.

In 1982 we didn't know what was causing the deadly new disease that newspapers began calling GRID, Gay-Related Immune Deficiency. About the same time that scientists isolated the HIV retrovirus, attendance at our dungeon parties had dwindled, and we eventually closed the clubhouse in May 1982. We continued to hold monthly play parties at other venues, however. Men whose partners were dying came not only to play, but also for brotherhood and mutual support. We continued to play to confront the devil, even if the evil could not be vanquished.

The exuberant mood of the previous decade turned to sober reflection. Discussions at The 15 Association meetings turned to how we might make our parties safer and lessen the spread of AIDS. Without knowledge, we were making guesses.

Even after the virus was identified, we didn't know how it spread. At one early meeting we discussed banning whipping, because the virus might be spread in the air from sweat and blood. We decided to eliminate piss play and got rid of the bathtub, even though in retrospect it was among the safest activities. Sex lessened at the parties, and in time there were bowls of condoms on tables.

We all became involved in fighting the disease as our friends and brothers fell ill. One of the first men stricken was our chairman, David Lewis. We raised money so that he and his partner Chump could go back to British Columbia to be with family and friends. He later recorded his death on a tape that was played on Public Radio. Very soon after founding member Charles Durham, an African-American, was chosen as the second chairman, he came down with the disease. In 1984 AIDS was a death sentence. In despair he took a taxi to the Golden Gate Bridge and jumped off.

After we closed the clubhouse, we continued to hold play parties at a dungeon rented from the Knights Templar, another BDSM group that was active for a short time in San Francisco. Paradoxically, even as AIDS decimated our membership, it strengthened those of us who survived. Our brotherhood was put to the test. We supported each other and became closer friends. Though the membership had fallen to seventy-five by 1985, I was by then a Fraternal, determined to keep the club alive through the dark times. I became the Activities Coordinator in 1985, and with considerable help from my brothers, organized the first Bootcamp, a weekend encampment of leathermen who played and ate together. This yearly event today draws over 100 men.

We survived this terrible time because we were more than a sex club: we were a brotherhood. We allowed men to play as they liked, wearing leather and boots, or jeans and sandals, or no clothes at all. We facilitated each other's fantasies and dreams, insisting on safety, but never being judgmental about the fetishes of others.

My early leather life of exploration was a time of great personal growth and a wonderful celebration of my sexuality as a gay man. But my leather life took on a greater meaning through the friendships that I've formed with my leather brothers throughout the world. My service to The 15 Association alongside my brothers past and present has been my greatest joy. I still love celebrating my leather life in play, but I am most proud of helping to create a community of gay leathermen that will last far into the future, even as generations to come adapt it for their own needs and purposes.

EPILOGUE
by Peter Fiske

I am the Everyman in Leather. If you look at leather history since 1964, I have had the honor of being near the center of it for over fifty years. I have lived, loved, mourned, fought, laughed, and played through most of our leather history. Occasionally, I have helped make it. The story of my life and loves is the Everyman story of a leather life lived at the vortex.

Although these memoirs end with the founding of The 15 Association, my leather life has continued to this day and will continue into the future. In June 1983 I first saw photos of the new International Mr. Leather, Coulter "Colt" Thomas. He fascinated me, and I was smitten by just his photograph. Coulter came to San Francisco for Gay Pride, riding on the Arena bar truck with Luke Daniel and many other hot leathermen. I was volunteering for the Aids Emergency Fund, working closely with Daddy Alan Selby to produce fundraising events. Alan came up with the ingenious concept of a San Francisco Leather Daddy & Leather Daddy's boy contest.

The first Leather Daddy contest took place that July 4th weekend at the SF Eagle and was a huge success. The Leather Daddy's boy contest followed over Labor Day. Colt Thomas and porn legend Al Parker were announced as judges, so I was excited when Daddy Alan asked me to work the event. I knew I would be meeting Colt and Al.

I arrived at 1:00 p.m. to set up for the beer bust. About an hour later Colt Thomas, his partner Charlie Smith, and Al Parker arrived together. My heart jumped, and I felt an electric surge of ecstasy when introduced to Colt. He noticed it too. Charlie and Al were amazingly beautiful as well, and I was thrilled to spend the day with all of them. With Daddy Alan and his husband Peter passing a joint, we were all laughing, joking, flirting, and having so much fun.

Colt was absolutely stunning, wearing a cut-off Levi-style leather jacket, leather pants, and highly polished police boots. He was a bit shy and soft spoken with a lively, eager, intelligent mind and a sweet disposition. Colt was the most beautiful man I had ever laid eyes on. I later wrote in the *International Mr. Leather Book of Champions,*

> He was a twenty-year-old medical intern at the University of Texas Galveston when he stepped onto the stage at IML and won the title of International Mr. Leather 1983. He radiated sex. Although he was only five feet nine inches tall, his chest and butt were perfection, so people didn't much notice or care that he was not tall. He was a sunny blond. He was a doctor, a cowboy, and a leatherman. He was every Daddy's boy and every Top's bottom. He was classy and better yet, he had class.

I have two photographs of that day taken by Robert Pruzan, a major Leather photographer of 1980s. In one Colt, Charlie, and Al Parker pose side by side. In the other the IML winners for 1982, 1983, and 1984 — Luke Daniel, Colt Thomas, and Ron Moore — smile at Robert's camera.

The SF Eagle was packed tight with over 2,000 men and women. It was so crowded that the contestants were interviewed on the roof of the annex bar. For eight dollars you got fried chicken, beans, and potato salad, with all the beer you could drink. The whole day is so bright in my memory that it could have been yesterday.

Epilogue 141

I knew Colt was with Charlie Smith, the love of his life. I also knew Colt was the love of my life. I accepted my place as a friend; it was enough. All I wanted was to be with Colt and Charlie and Al Parker. Al was incredibly sexy — he and his bent dick. We laughed and smoked and raised over $4,000 for AIDS Emergency Fund, enough for seven grants. Today as I look back on it, it is beyond a doubt the happiest day of my life.

Little did I know that four years later I would be with Coulter and that he would need all my love and support. In December 1986 Charlie Smith passed away in Detroit, where he and Coulter lived. Charlie was in isolation and not given enough pain medication. When Coulter, a resident at Wayne State University's Detroit Medical Center, objected, he was told, "You are nothing to this man and you work here. Butt out." Coulter struggled on for another year in medicine then quit. He phoned Daddy Alan Selby, who owned Mr. S Leather, and asked for a job. Alan said "yes" and in January 1988 Coulter moved to San Francisco.

That March I saw a notice in the *Bay Area Reporter* for an AIDS Emergency Fund benefit at the Eagle and agreed to help out. At the event I bought a signed 12 x 16 photograph and the t-shirt right off Coulter's back. Then I told Coulter that I loved him. He was taken aback and went over to ask Don Folkers, "Is he serious? Does he mean it? Is he crazy?" Don said, "Peter isn't crazy. He means every word seriously, and if you ever hurt him, I will come for you."

The four years we had together from March 20, 1988, to September 6, 1992, were the happiest years of my life. We lived together for three of those years. We traveled the world, and I took care of him. In 1989 Coulter told me in the elevator of the Hamilton Condos that he was sick and without a friend, that no one would ever love him again and he would die alone. He cried on my shoulder. I said, "I will love you, take care of you, and be your friend. You will not die alone." Coulter never hurt me or disappointed me. That day in 1989 was the start of the only true love that I have ever known, before or since.

Coulter loved his life while he was with me. He had so many friends and so much support. Our circle included Sky Renfrew, Shadow Morton, and Mike Hernandez — all still around and still close friends. He loved traveling, so we went to Europe twice and to Australia. In May 1991 he took me to my first IML. We shared a large suite with Sky, Shadow, Mike, and Jenny at the sleazy Chicago Congress Hotel. It was in and out sex and play, non-stop.

Coulter loved life in San Francisco. He loved dancing, music, working out, the bars, and Ringold Alley when the bars closed. Our favorite movie was *Steel Magnolias* where Julia Roberts says, "I'd rather have a short time of absolutely wonderful than a whole lifetime of nothing special." Coulter was my "absolutely wonderful." He lives on in me, and his light shines bright in my heart even now, twenty-seven years after he left me.

I feel Coulter and Charlie every day. I continue to live life fully and serve the community as they did. There is so much joy and play in my life because Coulter loved me. There is also a sadness and sense of loss there that never goes away. Coulter and Charlie were only two of the tens of thousands we lost in the plague years. As long as we remember them they are not silent. They lived. They loved. We remember the love, and life goes on.

In 1984 I attended my first Inferno and joined the Chicago Hellfire Club. The 15 Association had our first runs in Petaluma, California, in 1983, and then again in 1984 at Abel's Chicken Ranch. The 15 had monthly parties, which still continue today. In the midst of death and sorrow there was life and love, and what we did in San Francisco became a model for other cities. The leather community grew up. My years with the Hellfire Club were some of the best and hottest times I have ever had. As I evolved, I became primarily a Top. My whip collection had room to expand in my newly purchased condominium at 631 O'Farrell Street, where I lived for thirty years. I was still bottoming occasionally, and my favorite play partner was then an officer with the San Francisco Police. We still play, but now I am more likely to top Dick the Cop.

I became proficient in whip use and collected David Morgan bullwhips and quirts. Fred Katz brought long whips to Inferno, and I helped popularize them there and at The 15 Association. I also introduced single tail whips at Delta's annual run in the 90s. I became a member of The 15 Fraternal Committee in 1984 and continued volunteering with the Aids Emergency Fund. I also went on some actions with Act Up SF including the 1983 AIDS Conference and the 1984 Democratic National Convention, where we shut down rush hour traffic on Market Street and took over a cable car.

After Coulter Thomas left this world to be with his Charlie in 1992, I got busy and became an educator, a Board member of the Aids Emergency Fund, and then Vice-Chairman and Chairman of The 15. In the late 80s Coulter had introduced me to many men who were trans. I loved being with them and am still close with many including my chosen brother Billy Lane. In 1996 I was presented the Caligula Award by Chicago Hellfire Club at Inferno XXV. That was also the year Delta International had its first annual run.

I served on the AIDS Emergency Fund Board of Directors from 1997 to 2002 and was elected its President in 2000. Along with Mama Sandy Reinhardt and others we co-founded the Breast Cancer Emergency Fund in 2001. I served on the SF LGBT Pride Board from 2002 to 2005, and in that year was given the 2005 Pride Heritage Award for my over fifteen years of service to the San Francisco LGBT community. I was awarded two Pantheon of Leather Awards including Lifetime Achievement.

From 1995 to 2010 my sub was Charles Beck. The Leather Archives and Museum has his diary and photos of his beatings. I was attending every Inferno, most Deltas, and all The 15 Association Bootcamp runs. At these and other events, I was playing, mentoring, and teaching.

Tony DeBlase was first to champion the inclusion of trans men at Inferno in 1996; however, their acceptance to the annual run or other Hellfire events was refused. By 2003 I spoke with Billy Lane, and we decided to try again. By then, Delta International had been open to trans men since 1998, and the 15 Association had voted sixty-eight to one in 2002 to welcome men who are trans. In addition, Seattle Men in Leather also had an inclusive policy. Sadly, after Billy attended Inferno once in 2004, the Chicago Hellfire Club decided to close its doors to trans men. Thankfully, the men's leather community, including CHC and every other men's BDSM group in the US, has evolved over the last fifteen years, and all clubs now accept trans men as our brothers, with inclusive attendance and membership policies.

During this time from the 1980s until now I became active as a presenter at leather events and clubs, now well over a hundred events. I love sharing my knowledge and craft, and enjoy mentoring those who ask for help. My whip collection grew and grew and has become known as "the Peter Fiske Collection." I was given the honor of judging IML in the twenty-fifth anniversary year and then was asked to volunteer with the judges' staff, which I still do most years.

My infamous whip collection now has over 1000 whips, and just keeping them greased up and ready to use is quite a job. I continue with Delta International as a member, where I served as a board member and as Chairman and Run Coordinator in 2009 and 2010. I am also a member of Palm Springs Leather Order of the Desert, having moved to Palm Springs, California, in 2009, after having lived in San Francisco forty-three years. I was also a former longtime member of the now defunct clubs GMSMA (Gay Male SM Activists) and SNC (Sixty Nine Club) London and was a member of Chicago Hellfire Club from 1984 to 2006.

Two of my greatest honors were induction into the Leather Hall of Fame in 2017 and receiving the National LGBTQ Task Force's Leather Leadership Award in 2019.

I remember all the faces of the men and women I have known in leather these past fifty-three years. The young rebellious faces of the outlaw 60s, the wild ones of the love generation 70s, the classic leather-dressed faces of the 80s and 90s, and the new faces of a more diverse community of the new millennium. Men and women, singles and couples, the old guard, the new guard, and the no guard, Daddies and boys, Masters and slaves, Doms and subs, pups and handlers, fetishists, kinksters — all rich in life and love. I hope that our generation leaves growth, strength, acceptance, and change to the future generations, so that all can be themselves. We have come a long way from Marlon Brando and *The Wild One* and the Satyrs in 1954 Los Angeles.

Leather and BDSM have been more than a scene for me. They are my life and have given my whole life focus and direction. I care about the future and the men and women coming into the scene, and what they will find and create. I have many wonderful memories of all the people who have been with me, and I will go on playing and loving and teaching with gusto and joy for as long as I can. My advice to all who read my memoirs: Live large. Play hard. Love with all your might. Be the friend you want to have. Always tip your bartenders and bootblacks well, and support the Leather Archives and Museum.

www.ingramcontent.com/pod-product-compliance
Lightning Source LLC
Chambersburg PA
CBHW020424010526
44118CB00010B/416